DO IT WITH PASSION

OR NOT AT ALL!

CNC
LAS

LA
LAS
LAS
PLAN

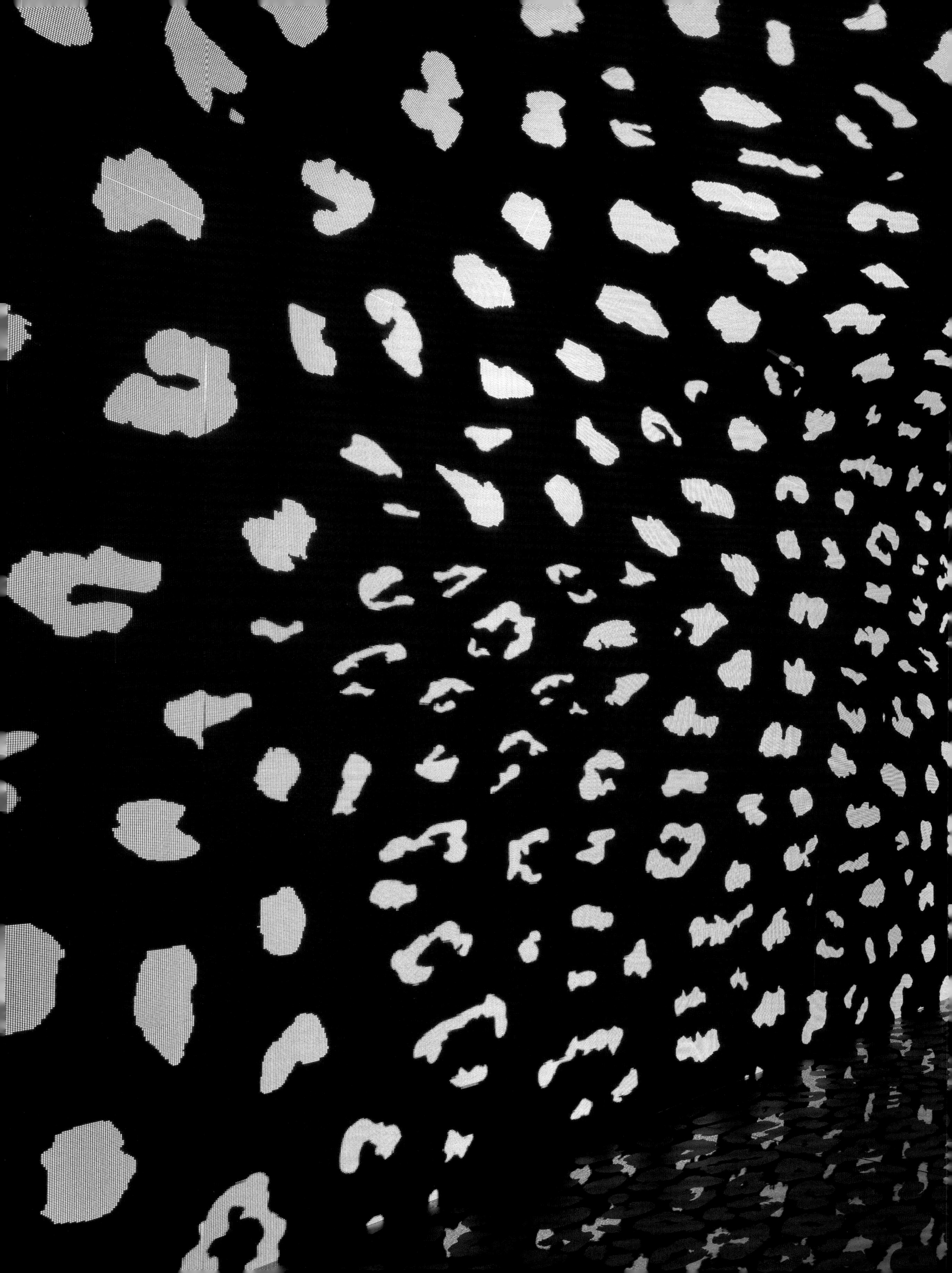

L'ATELIER FIVE

CONTAGIOUS CREATIVITY

images
Publishing

THE PERFUMERY HALL

CONTENTS

LAS
LAS
LAS
LAS

THE ALCHEMIST

Push open the gleaming doors of a luxury retailer, and you step into a world of curated elegance designed to captivate the senses and transport you into a realm of exclusivity. Each element, from installations to the lighting, is precisely placed and calibrated to create an atmosphere with that elusive—yet all-important and instantly recognisable—'immersive' quality that makes the brand enticing, enchanting, magical. Suddenly, you've got to have that cream, that jewel, that handbag, that sweater, that life.

Behind the imposing façades are magicians of a sort, a hardworking team led by a singularly driven dreamer and do-er: Saina Attaoui. Self-started and self-made, Saina this year celebrates the tenth anniversary of L'Atelier Five in London, and the fifth of its office in Dubai. She launched this unique, award-winning design agency solo, from scratch, in 2015. What she lacked, utterly, in terms of financing and industry connections, she compensated for with mettle, pluck, determination, a sure eye and unerring taste, plus a dash of improv as needed.

L'Atelier Five's founder and managing director, Saina operates like an alchemist in her own right, investing luxury's dazzling opulence with experiences that are tailored to resonate on an emotional level. "The luxury industry is about selling dreams, not just products," she notes. That philosophy underpins everything L'Atelier Five does, from designing shelving to curating retail experiences.

As the invisible hand behind the luxurious client experience, Saina specialises in anything a brand might refer to as a 'special project' or, in current parlance, 'activation.' These may include collaborations, temporary installations like pop-up stores, travel retail happenings and 'take-overs'—in which a brand confers its identity on an existing retailer, such as Harrods—or creating digital content to build followings and reach new clienteles. From dreaming up bespoke settings for iconic jewellers such as Cartier at Selfridges, Harrods and in Saudi Arabia, to elevating the perception of watches, beauty and high-end spirits in travel hubs or other high-traffic environments, and creating an actual gingerbread finish for the "Fabulous World of Dior" Christmas takeover at Harrods, L'Atelier Five has become a byword for creativity, precision, resourcefulness and a flair for perfectly reflecting each brand's image, wherever the setting.

"Saina is definitely all about creating a collaborative, family-style environment. We're encouraged to work closely together and brainstorm together. And, we support each other when there are challenges. We get each other through the difficulties."

Jasmine Bagaria, Head of Creative, L'Atelier Five

When the Doors Close, the Magic Begins

Behind the glamorous storefronts and glittering showcases, away from the public eye, Saina and her team work like elves in a business where every day is like Christmas morning.

"Once the last customer leaves and the doors shut for the evening, a whole secret world comes to life," she recounts. "That's when we move in and get to work, often through the night, pouring our blood, sweat and tears into crafting the magic and emotion."

In lieu of a magic wand, there are the designers, carpenters, electricians, painters and artists wielding blueprints, hammers, cables, glue guns, brushes and paint to make a brand's vision a reality, often under tight deadlines and stringent budgets. Yet with every new project, the thrill of leaving indelible impressions lets the team look at the world with fresh eyes all over again.

As dynamic as it is exclusive, the luxury retail industry is constantly under pressure, buffeted by geopolitical crosswinds and constantly shifting market demands. Transforming her personal characteristics into professional assets, Saina fashioned L'Atelier Five for speed and suppleness so that it could adapt and innovate amid a challenging environment. Her client roster is a testament to her foresight and resilience: whether it's creating an experiential pop-up for Tiffany & Co., or designing a high-profile collaboration for a legacy watchmaker like Audemars Piguet, the agency's portfolio reflects unparalleled versatility as well as an uncompromising level of taste.

Even so, L'Atelier Five's work surpasses aesthetics: it's about creating emotional connections. Each project is tailored to evoke a feeling, tell a story and leave a lasting impact. That approach has earned L'Atelier Five industry accolades and the enduring trust of some of the world's most discerning brands, who rely on the agency not just to deliver but to delight.

In an industry rife with creative agencies, L'Atelier Five opts to operate artisanally, hewing to a hands-on philosophy that puts it in a league of its own. "Ours is a small, family-style 'one-stop shop' kind of agency," Saina explains. From design and conception to delivery and installation and every single step along the way, it's hands-on—a comprehensive approach that extends to dismantling and responsible waste disposal, thus ensuring that every aspect of a project is handled mindfully.

"As a single mum, to set up in business and go on and become an international design agency is no mean feat. Saina has shaken things up and she is known in London and Dubai as someone who stands by her word and delivers."

Richard Heighes, former business partner

Boutique Precision, Global Reach

Though headquartered in London, L'Atelier Five has expanded to include production facilities in Windsor, United Kingdom, and a satellite office in Dubai to ensure a truly global reach. In London, Paris, Seoul and Singapore, as in Riyadh, Kuala Lumpur and Monaco—amongst many other ports of call—Saina and her team have earned a reputation for bringing a brand's vision to life in any context. Inevitably, that implies a heavy travel schedule to ensure that execution meets her exacting standards. "I'm a modern nomad," Saina says with a laugh.

But while Saina's drive, hands-on leadership and attention to detail are the cornerstones of her success, L'Atelier Five also reflects its founder's journey from a modest upbringing in rural France to the cosmopolitan heart of London, from budding creative to founder of one of the industry's most respected boutique agencies. Her story is one of determination, resilience, and a deep understanding of people and brands. But it is her level of dedication—to both her clients and her teams—that sets L'Atelier Five apart.

A Philosophy Rooted in Craftsmanship

Saina describes L'Atelier Five as more an artisanal workshop than a corporate entity. The agency operates like a family, with each team member bringing unique expertise to the table. Designers envision the creative blueprint, project managers oversee the intricacies of logistics and production teams bring the vision to life. It's a seamless collaboration in which every role is essential, and every detail matters.

That approach extends to the execution of projects, which are handled with the utmost care and precision. From the initial sketches to the final installation, L'Atelier Five's work reflects a commitment to craftsmanship that is rare in today's fast-paced world. "We don't just design and build; we craft," Saina emphasises. That ethos resonates with the company's luxury clients, who value the agency's ability to make their vision a reality with both authenticity and flair. "We specialise in delivering the kind of projects few can execute," Saina says with justifiable pride.

"When Saina launched her own company, I wanted to give her a chance because of her drive. With Saina, nothing was impossible. She has this willpower to do the impossible."

Natacha Prihnenko, Director of Window Display Development, Hermès (1990–2021)

The Future of Luxury

As the luxury industry continues to evolve with unprecedented speed, L'Atelier Five continues to innovate and adapt to new trends and challenges. Not content to just maintain the status quo, Saina intends to keep pushing the boundaries of what is possible in luxury retail design, from incorporating new-gen tech to exploring ever-more sustainable practices in design and production. As experience has shown, the relentless pursuit of excellence, combined with a habit of dreaming big, consistently results in something extraordinary.

"The pursuit of excellence is about pleasing others, but it's also about pleasing herself. [It's about] the satisfaction of a job well done."

Claire Meyssan, Special Projects Senior Manager, Cartier

CHRIST
CHRISTIAN DIOR
CHRISTIAN DIOR

AN DIOR
CHRISTIAN DIOR

CNC
LA 5

AN OUTSIDER

The modern luxury industry traces its roots all the way back to the royal courts of Europe. And, while it has gradually grown beyond aristocratic circles over the centuries, it remains even today, a stubbornly exclusive 'club.' Dominated by a handful of luxury conglomerates, each with their own carefully cultivated networks, recruitment rarely strays from a handful of exclusive business schools and well-connected recruiters act as the industry's gatekeepers. So it goes for the creative agencies that cater to luxury brands as well. L ttle opportunity is left for outsiders, let alone someone entirely self-made. Every so often, however, a wild card comes along and forces the industry to take note.

The daughter of Moroccan immigrants raised in a caretaker's cottage on the grounds of a château in rural Normandy, Saina Attaoui's professional journey began far removed from the glossy world of luxury. In fact, her first job was selling accessories for the quintessential toy for boys: motorbikes. The only woman member of the sales team of a motorbike chain in the south of France, the fit was hardly an obvious one. "I went out and got all the books I could find on motorbikes and studied them until I knew more about motorbikes than any of my male colleagues," recalls Saina. "I even learned how to drive one. And I loved it!" Her pluck took her next to Monaco where she sold high-end building fixtures, followed by a stint in retail and merchandising at a jewellery brand and eventually, she tried her hand at importing Berbère crafts for sale in markets around the south of France.

Dissatisfied with the professional landscape in France and looking for new challenges, she moved to London armed with little more than a rudimentary grasp of English and no professional network to fall back on. "I knew no one so I used to go to pubs alone and strike up a conversation with other patrons," she recalls. "Then I would go home and look up the new words I'd heard at the pub." After a brief stint on the sales floor of a high-end boutique to perfect her English, she ventured into the world of entrepreneurship, opening a sales agency in East London where she sold fashion accessories for a while. "I didn't make a lot but at least I didn't owe the government any money when I closed down the business," she quips.

> "She was a salesperson at the time; I told her she should set up in business. I thought she had a lot to offer the industry if she started out for herself. I suppose I saw something about her that reminded me of my younger self, fifteen years earlier."
>
> Richard Heighes, former business partner

Saina eventually landed at a creative agency where she learned the ropes of the luxury industry. Drawn to the luxury world for its rich history and evocative storytelling, she quickly built up an impressive book of business and developed key relationships, deepening her knowledge of the industry along the way. Natacha Prihnenko, then Director of Window Display Development at Hermès, recalls their first interactions. "With Saina, nothing was impossible. She has this willpower to do the impossible." Prihnenko had been particularly impressed with Saina's ability to produce results even on challenging projects, explaining, "Sometimes it was difficult to produce the creative concepts that we wanted. Saina managed to get our messages across in a very fluid, efficient way, despite the budgetary constraints and obstacles. Her personality is formed by determination."

That unique determination to overcome virtually any obstacle in her way to produce innovative concepts, delivered on time and in accordance with exacting client specs, became her signature and she soon made a name for herself with other luxury brands. "People have a great deal of respect for her because she's a bit of a dark horse," explains Sarah Metalnikoff, Operations Manager at L'Atelier Five in Dubai, adding, "Saina doesn't think like everybody else. She looks at things and approaches them in her own unique way." "Even very early on, I wasn't interested in going to work for the big luxury brands," reflects Saina. "I would have been made to fit a box and I didn't want that. I know that who I am, my personality and what I stand for is probably what has gotten me here today."

It wasn't long however before a familiar restlessness set in. "I was frustrated and wanted to stamp my mark, I wanted to build something of my own," she recalls. Richard Heighes, a former collaborator and friend, was one of the first to encourage her to venture out on her own. "I think she was surprised," reflects Heighes. "A lot of people who are passionate about what they do need to step back and take a helicopter view. Taking that leap into the unknown is not easy."

WURTH

THE PERFECT
GIFT

OHNNIE WALKER
GLETON
JOHNNIE WALKER
Blue Label
XORDINAIRE
BLENDED SCOTCH
JOHNNIE WALKER
Blue Label
Blue Label
XORDINAIRE
TRAVEL
EXCLUSIVE

AN ENTREPRENEUR

In 2015, Saina Attaoui took the plunge and founded L'Atelier Five. Some entrepreneurs are careful to have a Plan B, a safety net to cushion a possible fall. For Saina, however, that was not an option. "My only 'Plan B' was to move back in with my mother and sleep on her sofa," recalls Saina jokingly. Luckily, what she did have in add tion to her signature determination was the confidence and support of true believers, a diverse cast of individuals who had seen her in action and knew instinctively that if anyone could pull it off, she could. Richard Heighes certainly thought she had what it takes and was willing to put up the seed money to prove it. When asked what made him think that Saina had the mettle, he explains: "To run a business, you need an armour-plated suit ... you have to be able to brush off detractors and stand up in a room and say you can do this and be better than your competitors. Saina has all that."

Still, her armour-plated suit aside, the first few years of L'Atelier Five were lean. Claire Thirion, then a freelance creative designer who joined Saina on the fledgling agency's very first project pitch, remembers, "At the time, Saina had rented an office in this tiny street in SoHo where sex workers hung out. It was a funny contrast with the level of project we were working on and the level of client." The client in question was Hermès no less and L'Atelier Five went on to win that pitch, and many more after that. Sophie Quilling, the agency's first permanent employee, recalls the tremendous pressure carried by Saina in those early days: "Landing clients, recruiting staff, making payroll; it must have been stressful, yet she never showed it. Even in the face of setbacks, she just kept going. I find that really inspirational." The early years of L'Atelier Five were challenging, acknowledges Heighes. "But Saina never lost belief in the goal, and she wound up shaking up a very established industry," he notes admiringly. Within the first year of founding L'Atelier Five, the agency actually managed to break even, unusual for start-ups known for burning through cash for years before finally reaching profitability. "Everything we earned was injected back into the business. More importantly, we had grown exclusively by word of mouth," recalls Saina proudly. Given the fierce competition among well-established players, the accomplishment is far from modest. L'Atelier Five, a tiny start-up led by a woman with no gold-plated credentials, was upsetting the apple cart one show-stopping project at a time. The luxury industry sat up and took note.

> "To run a business, you need an armour-plated suit, you need 100 percent confidence in what you do, you have to be able to brush off detractors and stand up in a room and say you can do this and be better than your competitors. Saina has all that."
>
> Richard Heighes, former business partner

As L'Atelier Five grew in stature, so too did the pressure to deliver the level of service that luxury brands typically expect of agencies. Staffing is always crucial, especially for a start-up. In the early days, the agency relied essentially on a changing cast of talented freelance creatives and project managers to deliver the magic. Saina herself had no qualms about picking up a hammer or glue gun when the situation required it. "Saina has never been afraid to get her hands dirty," recalls Quilling. "During long nights of installing displays, she would be right there alongside the production team. That means a lot." Charlotte Adam, one of L'Atelier Five's former project managers, agrees, adding: "She's the CEO but, if there is a problem, she will step in to support her team. She's not sitting in her office, inaccessible."

As it turns out, Saina is also not afraid to charm perfect strangers into lending a hand when the occasion calls for it. During one particularly challenging project in Geneva, the team was under a tight deadline and grappling with a tricky installation. She stepped out to buy dinner for her team at the local supermarket where she chanced upon two craftsmen finishing up for the day. After a brief conversation over the bread aisle, she managed to persuade them to come lend a hand. Thanks to a bit of serendipity and the kindness of two random strangers, the tricky installation was completed on time and to the exact specifications of the client. "Flying in the face of adversity is one of Saina's greatest skills," suggests Heighes. "She is unflappable."

Even after a decade of growth and success, however, the life of an entrepreneur can still sometimes feel like a high-wire act. "I'm scared virtually every single day but if I were to focus on that, I wouldn't be able to move forward," says Saina matter-of-factly, "so I just crack on with it. I believe positive energy attracts positive outcomes."

DUBAI
WONDER
CLASH de Cartier

LAS

MATERIALS
BOARD

AN INNOVATOR

Our culture venerates innovation. We celebrate the tech industry for its 'disruptive technologies' that transform the way we work. We celebrate medical breakthroughs that transform the way we live. Yet, we rarely acknowledge innovative leadership, the kind that draws on compassion and respect to elevate others and enable them to express the best versions of themselves. After a decade, L'Atelier Five stands out not least because this tiny, family-style agency is transforming the way luxury brands engage with consumers but is doing so thanks to the innovative leadership of one woman determined to do it differently.

The world of creative agencies, like the luxury industry itself, remains male-dominated even today. Determined from the start to achieve success on her own terms, Saina Attaoui traced a very different path for her agency. "I didn't build up my agency to get rich," she explains. "I want to be profitable obviously, but I also want it to be an enjoyable journey, for my clients, for my team and for myself." She openly acknowledges that both her entrepreneurial vision and her leadership style are a product, at least in part, of being a woman: 'As women, there is a clear emotional aspect to how we drive our business. We want to thrive and grow, certainly, but the goal is not to eliminate everyone else."

Her approach, even today, remains surprisingly unorthodox. And, in the cut-throat world of creative agencies, it sticks out, especially among clients. As Hermès' Natacha Prihnenko observes: "With L'Atelier Five, Saina had the ambition to create more of a family than a business. She has a way of making others comfortable, which makes them want to work with her." "Clients see her pouring her heart into her projects and they see how she treats her team," confirms former project manager, Charlotte Adam. "They respond to her warmth and generosity." And, perhaps because Saina herself pours her heart and soul into every project, it makes her team want to go the extra mile themselves. Claire Meyssan, Special Projects Senior Manager at Cartier, echoes that sentiment: "L'Atelier Five is really a part of her. You sense that she manages her team like a family, and you can feel that as a result, they're happy to go even farther for her." "She's really good at knowing how to push her team beyond their comfort zone and getting them to execute her vision," confirms Sophie Quilling. "She brings out the best in them."

"A great project isn't just about one thing—it's about many small aspects coming together. If you miss even one, it won't be at the level you want. Saina understands that."

Luca Albero, Visual Merchandising Creation and Image Director, Dior

Saina's innovative leadership style doesn't just enable her to get the best out of her team. That peculiar brand of energy, that extra spark she brings, enables her to execute projects that elevate the luxury consumer experience and set new standards for the industry. If proof of concept is required, one need only look to L'Atelier Five's early track record. When Luca Albero, Dior's Visual Merchandising Creation and Image Director, assembled a team of partners including the fledgling agency for an experimental retail activation project at Harrods in 2018, he was acutely aware that they were navigating unchartered waters: "It was the beginning of a new approach. Today, experiential retail is common but back then it marked a real shift," he recalls. "We were experimenting. There was a lot of pressure. But it changed the industry." When a luxury sector leader like Dior recruits a tiny start-up agency to help launch a cutting-edge retail activation concept, it doesn't go unnoticed. "Saina has the ability to put you at ease because you know that she'll find a solution," recalls Albero. "Others saw what we did at Harrods and said, 'let's try this too!' We moved the industry forward."

Like all confident leaders, Saina is quick to acknowledge the contribution of others. "From the very beginning, I felt very deeply that as a woman, I was being supported by other women in the industry." And so, she has made a point of paying it forward. The world of creative agencies is more diverse today not just for her unique brand of leadership but also for her mentorship of others. Claire Thirion, a collaborator from the early days of L'Atelier Five and now at the helm of her own London-based creative agency, explains: "There aren't many women at our senior level, so we always have each other's backs. Saina is exactly the kind of person who's there for you whenever you need her." Similarly, Stephanie Paris, a former designer for L'Atelier Five, values the lessons learned from Saina at the start of her career. "She helped me hone my creativity while developing my management skills. I continue to build on that foundation even today." When asked why mentoring others matters to her, Saina answers simply: "Success at business is one thing but raising others up along the way is much more rewarding."

DIOR
CHRISTIAN DIOR

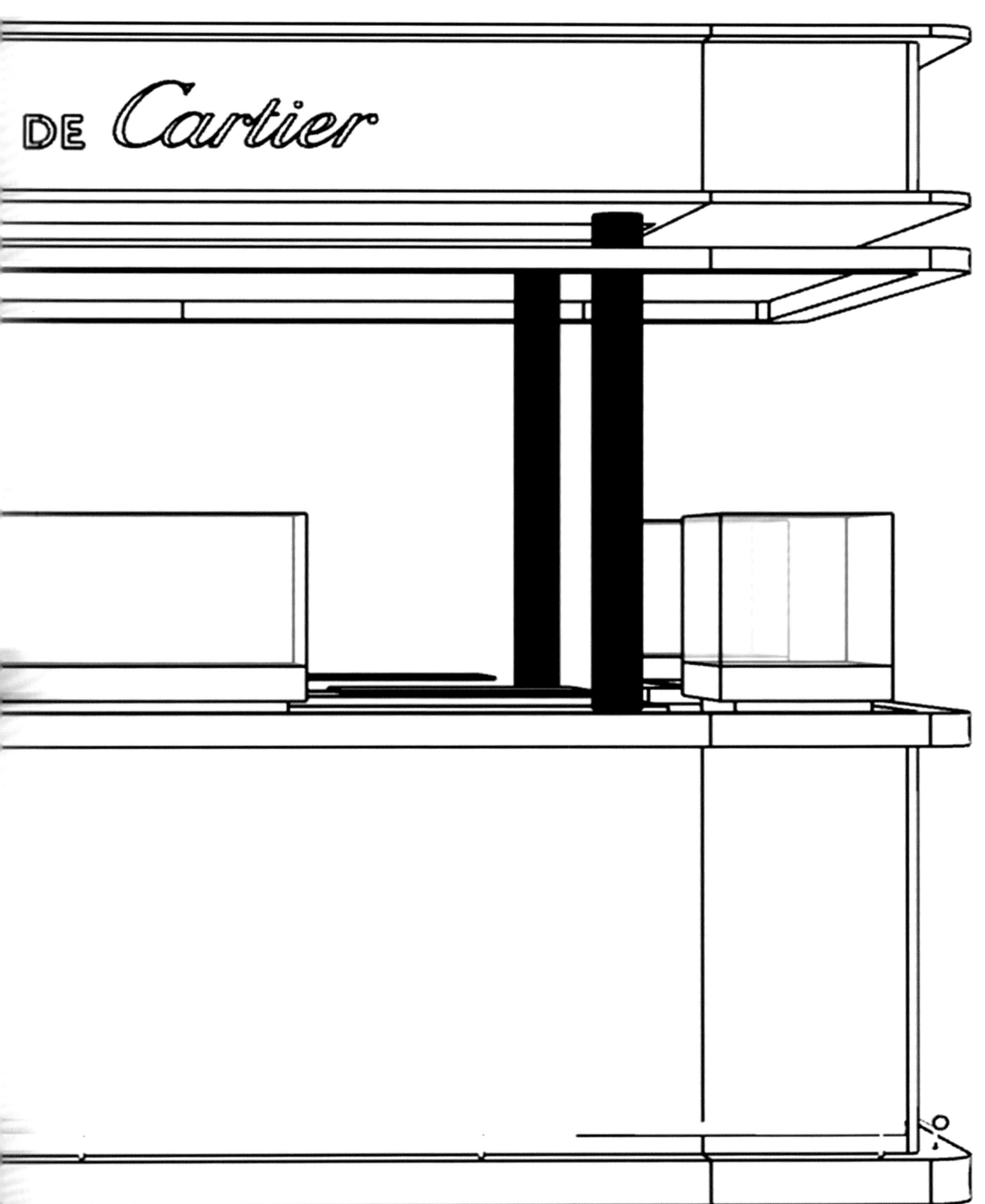
DE Cartier

ON
OFF
ON
OFF

A CREATIVE

Creativity is a frequently misunderstood concept, one our culture tends to define narrowly and commonly reduces to 'the arts.' A songwriter is obviously creative. So too is a painter or filmmaker. Often overlooked however is the role of creativity as a tool for everyday problem solving. It's hardly surprising therefore that many creatives fail to recognise this particular talent in themselves even when it's an essential skill they deploy on a regular basis.

"For the longest time, I didn't consider myself as creative," muses Saina Attaoui, "until one day I realised that being resourceful is a way of expressing creativity. And I'm quite good at being resourceful. In fact, I could not do what I do without being resourceful." This insight proved particularly useful when it came to structuring her own agency. From the beginning, Saina conceived of L'Atelier Five as a closely integrated platform to foster collaborative, family-style interactions where everyone is encouraged to brainstorm and work closely together. Famously averse to micromanagement, she allows her team the space to work through challenges together, stepping in only when she feels they require guidance.

The result is heightened awareness among her team of shared challenges and the ability to collaborate across disciplines more fluidly. "The transition from design to production is tricky," observes L'Atelier Five's Head of Creative, Jasmine Bagaria. "Designers can sometimes be a little too whimsical so the opportunity to work directly with our production partners for instance is especially insightful because we learn to adjust our designs and translate them into reality. It's a good reminder that resourcefulness is an important part of creativity."

In a crowded luxury market where brands all compete for a small pool of customers, the ability to capture attention and enchant is essential. "Ours is a very diluted industry," observes Bagaria. "Seemingly everything has been done already so coming up with something unique definitely requires resourcefulness." It sounds simple but creativity and innovation don't just happen in the abstract.

> "It isn't enough for Saina to succeed by herself. She wants others to succeed too. She cares about whether you're growing in the business."
>
> Hallia Ait-Khelfa, Executive Coordinator & PA to MD, L'Atelier Five

One could argue that it takes a strong creative mind to manage a team of creatives effectively to bring a concept to life on time and within budget. As Dior's Luca Albero notes, "Creativity exists everywhere but making creativity a reality, that's not something just anyone can do. Saina really has a feel for projects and she knows how to improve them."

This particular approach to agency work is what has allowed L'Atelier Five to become the 'go to' agency for innovative concepts that take brand activations a level above the rest. "Over the years, I've built up trust with my clients such that they're willing to follow me when I suggest a direction they may not have considered," explains Saina. "We always try to present our clients with two or three directions," she adds. "There is the safer, more corporate direction, a more creative direction that nudges the brand a bit more out of its comfort zone and an intermediate direction." Renowned for its elaborate, bespoke installations involving painstakingly handcrafted elements, L'Atelier Five has a long record of collaborating with artists and artisans, a practice they're rightfully proud of. "Whenever we can, we like to work with local artists and craftspeople," explains Saina. "We've been doing that since we began nearly ten years ago." Today, the agency has an extensive network of artists and artisans from around the world they can call upon giving them a distinctive edge.

The trick of course is to keep the ideas flowing, for creativity of any kind requires nurturing and care. Remaining fresh and able to sustain the constant churn of a cut-throat industry requires a nimble mind. "My brain is never really switched off," admits Saina. "There's always something or someone to capture my interest. Sometimes it's a scientific breakthrough that has no obvious connection to the luxury industry but that can lead to a new way of thinking about a challenge. It might inspire me to think differently about something." When asked where her creativity and resourcefulness come from, she pauses. After a moment of reflection, she answers simply, "When you're born with little, but you have big dreams and big ambitions, that's when you need to get creative."

LAS
LAS
LAS
LAS

A SINGULAR PASSION

"A client once told me that my passion is contagious," recalls Saina Attaoui. "It resonated with me." And perhaps herein lies the secret ingredient of L'Atelier Five's success. Without passion, it's simply not possible to sustain and thrive in the midst of all the deadlines, competition and pressure. The pace alone would be enough to wear down even the most committed among us. Dior's Luca Albero probably puts it best when he says, "The only reason anyone works in this industry is passion. Otherwise, you wouldn't survive."

The truth about the luxury industry is that behind the glamour lies a complex set of harsh realities that intersect. Failing to grasp the connections can make the difference between a successful agency that consistently hits its marks and one that utterly flops. "Luxury is a very international field," notes Saina. "You need to understand politics, culture, religion and language. It's all interconnected and it not only impacts our projects but it affects our relationships with our clients so we need to keep on top of it."

Case in point: in 2020, Saina recognised the early signs of an industry shift towards the Middle East. Never one to sit back and wait for opportunities to materialise, she boarded a flight to Dubai to experience the vibes firsthand. Her gut told her it was worth a go. Little did she know at the time that the world was a few weeks away from being thrown off its axis by a global pandemic. Most people would have backed down and shelved the project until the situation returned to some semblance of normalcy. Of course, Saina is not like most people. "Some people follow their hearts," observes Sarah Metalnikoff, L'Atelier Five's Dubai Operations Manager, "Saina follows her gut, and once her mind is made up, that's it! This is what makes her so successful." "I opened our Dubai office just as the pandemic was unfolding," explains Saina. "Opening in Dubai is already a challenge but add to that the constraints of the pandemic! I was working every single day almost around the clock." But five years later and L'Atelier Five Dubai is an undeniable success enabling the agency to execute even the most complex projects seamlessly across the region and beyond.

> "Saina has an abundant energy to give to anything she does. She does everything with passion."
>
> Richard Heighes, former business partner

It's not just markets that shift but societal values as well. The luxury industry is frequently singled out for its wasteful practices, not a desirable look when you're courting a new generation of customers keen on pursuing a sustainable lifestyle. Closely attuned to these generational shifts, L'Atelier Five sought early on to implement more sustainable practices. "Long before sustainability became trendy, we were already very sensitive to the issue of waste in our industry," explains Saina. "Partly, it's because we work so hard to build everything from scratch and it's heartbreaking to have to destroy it afterwards." Recycling is a priority and every element of their installations are recycled once the project is completed, all at the agency's cost. Whenever possible, they try to reuse materials or donate various elements of the installations to art or drama schools. Where items are branded, however, like all agencies, they are contractually bound to destroy it. Slowly, and diplomatically, L'Atelier Five works to promote a more environmentally friendly approach to their clients. "We always strive to offer a sustainable option to our clients. But ultimately, it is their decision."

The pressure to keep up with the evolving industry forces and exacting standards expected of clients is relentless. As Albero puts it, "When I put a big project on the table, I prefer working with partners who fight for you. That's how you achieve something incredible." Of course, incredible achievements come at a cost and the toll exacted to meet these expectations is high. "Each time we complete a really big project, we look back and ask ourselves how we managed to get through it," acknowledges Saina. "Then we wonder how we'll ever top it. It's what drives us. It's what keeps the adrenaline going."

When asked how she manages to cope with it all, Saina reflects for a moment. "It's all a leap of faith," she says thoughtfully. "I understand that I may fail but I can't just give up in the middle of the process. It's like you realise you're in a tunnel but you can't just stop when you're in the middle. You've come too far to stop. You just have to keep going." As it turns out, it may not be passion alone that delivers L'Atelier Five's particular brand of magic but the alchemy produced when it meets its founder's signature determination.

LOUIS
L'ATELIER FIVE
LONDON—DUBAI

CARTIER

1900 - 1920

LECOULTRE MEETS JAEGER

In 1903, Paris-based watchmaker to the French Navy, Edmond Jaeger, challenges Swiss manufacturers to develop and produce the ultra-thin movements that he has invented. Jacques-David LeCoultre, Antoine's grandson who is responsible for production at LeCoultre & Cie., accepts the challenge.

THE ATMOS PATENT

In 1928, Jean-Léon Reutter develops the first clock with a semi-perpetual movement enabling the mechanism to wind itself. Reutter sells the Atmos patent to LeCoultre on July 27th 1935 and the technique, redesigned and improved by Jaeger-LeCoultre, endures today.

CALIBR…

Jaeger-LeCoultre craftsmen miniaturise the Duoplan movement to create the Calibre 101 – the smallest hand-wound mechanical calibre in the world consisting of 98 parts weighing barely one gram. It is still produced today.

1950

MEMOVOX

The first wristwatch in the world … alarm, Memovox – "the voice of … is initially designed to help busin… remember their meetings throug… function. "Memovox reminds, no… and wakes up" announces the firs…

1907

ULTRA-THIN CALIBRE

In 1907 LeCoultre & Cie create the Calibre 145, the thinnest movement in the world. Just 1.38 mm thick, it defies the laws of physics and all technical constraints, a record which remains unbroken for decades.

…3

…0

…TINY WORKSHOP …LL-FLEDGED …FACTURE

…toine LeCoultre, a blacksmith's son …cal pioneer, founds the first …oultre workshop. By 1866, …op is transformed into a full-fledged …e of advanced watchmaking complications, … & Cie.

1925 - 1935

ART DECO AND THE FIRST ICONS

The Twenties and Thirties remain synonymous with abundant creativity. In just a few years the Grande Maison develops an impressive number of instantly famous models, including the Duoplan calibre, the Atmos clock and the emblematic Reverso.

1980 - 1990

THE ADVENT OF COMPLICATION…

The latter yea…

In 1992, the new Master Colle[...] the 1,000 Hours Control, a quality check p[...] which now subjects finished watches to a battery of rigorous tests covering every aspect of performance of all watches produced by the Manufacture.

2007

DUOMÈTRE AND DUAL WING® CONCEPT

Inspired by an 1880 chronometer, the Dual-Wing concept invented by Jaeger-LeCoultre is revolutionary in two ways, as dual, yet independent, mechanisms united by a single r[...] organ provide the [...]

PROJECT PORTFOLIO

SAVANNAH HERMÈS

In 2016, we were approached by Hermès to work on a tribute to Robert Dallet, one of the house's long-standing artistic collaborators. First invited in 1985 by the then-president of Hermès, Jean-Louis Dumas, to design one of the house's iconic silk scarves, Dallet would go on to design no less than twenty-five scarves over more than two decades of collaboration along with many other accessories. It was his very first scarf design, the "Kenya," that would set the theme for this tribute. Working alongside Hermès' experienced Canadian production manager, we set out to transform Hermès' windows into an evocative African savannah landscape featured in international airports across four major North American cities in tribute to Dallet.

New York, San Francisco, Los Angeles and Vancouver Airports / 2016

This project involved the installation of windows at multiple airports and travel retail spaces. The intricate design featured 3D rope trees, a circular fabric-printed background, cracked texture flooring and 3D animal elements to evoke the rugged, arid beauty of the African savannah.

The Hermès window installation project marked a pivotal moment for us as an agency. It was both our first international project and our inaugural collaboration with a heritage luxury house. It laid the foundation for our future in global luxury retail design, proving that bold creativity paired with meticulous execution could open doors across continents. That a fledgling London-based design studio was commissioned to design Hermès' windows across major North American cities spoke volumes about our potential in the luxury retail sphere. It remains to this day a milestone in our studio's journey.

SPECIAL SELECTION AT INTERNATIONAL A' DESIGN AWARD & COMPETITION
BRONZE SELECTION
2018

WILD HORSES
HERMÈS

Here we were tasked with creating a culturally sensitive window display to attract and engage the viewer while forging a connection between the brand and the local culture. Kuwait is an arid country, surrounded by sandy dunes and desert landscapes. Horses have been both a means of travel and a source of income, playing a major part of daily life through the centuries up to the current day. The horse is also at the centre of Hermès' brand identity. It was therefore the perfect creature to capture the imagination of Kuwait City's inhabitants and forge an emotional connection between the brand and the city via the boutique's window displays.

Kuwait City / 2016

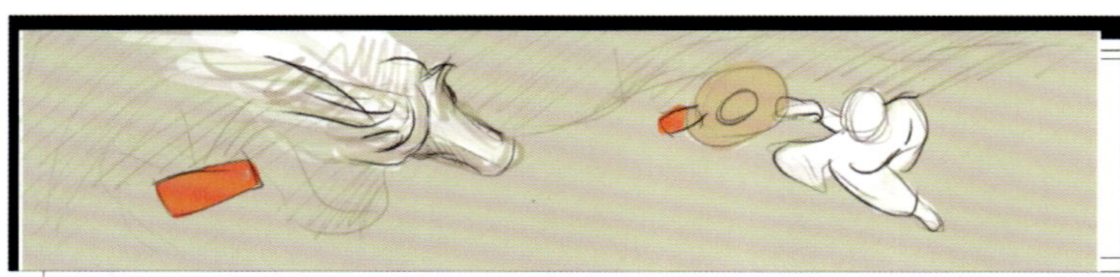

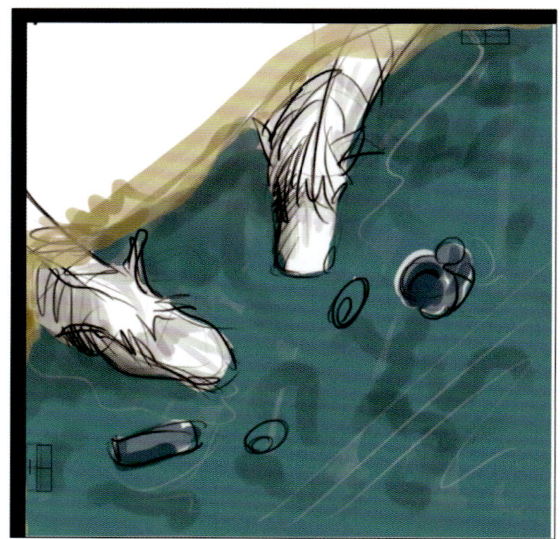

In order to play on the behaviour of the horse in its natural habitat, it was important that we showcase both the gentle nature of the animal and its considerable physical strength. The display was designed to take passing viewers on a scenic journey to witness the horse galloping wild through arid plains and eventually resting peacefully at a watering hole. The main aim was to keep the windows looking fluid and natural, which we achieved using natural grasses and realistic horse figures cast and moulded in fibreglass. The success of the window rested on our ability to create a realistic water effect for the watering hole in a tightly enclosed corner space offering only limited access. The designs were kept loose to avoid overcomplicating the production phase and the visual impact of the installation.

"Saina has a zest for life that not everyone has. It wouldn't be L'Atelier Five without her."

Sophie Quilling, Operations Manager 2016–2018, L'Atelier Five

“What influenced me most was Saina’s unstoppable ‘can-do’ attitude—she’s a true badass.”

Claire Thirion, freelance Creative Designer

HERMÈS

HERMÈS
HERMÈS

SPECIAL SELECTION AT INTERNATIONAL A' DESIGN AWARD & COMPETITION
SILVER SELECTION
2018

BLOOM AT NIGHT
ALEXANDER MCQUEEN

Our original brief was to create a dramatic haute couture–inspired narrative for the Alexander McQueen fragrance "Bloom at Night" and translate it into one single window display for the flagship Saks Fifth Avenue department store in Manhattan. The brief then swelled to three windows and would eventually culminate in a complete takeover of all Saks Fifth Avenue's flagship store windows.

Saks Fifth Avenue, New York City / 2016

Working in close collaboration with the Alexander McQueen brand, Saks Fifth Avenue and later Procter & Gamble, we devised a dramatic visual narrative around the fragrance's key notes: ylang ylang, tuberose and jasmine. Its conception alone required three months of meticulous design and development with each flower's rendering becoming a study in artistic innovation. The ylang ylang, initially rendered in hand-dyed yellow leather for Saks' exclusive launch, later evolved into white leather with delicate gold-brushed details for other markets. The tuberose emerged as a triumph of engineering and aesthetics involving layers of engraved polycarbonate, each bearing art deco details, hand-bent to achieve an organic fluidity. The jasmine, originally conceived in sugar paste and porcelain, required reimagining when its popularity engendered greater demand. After exploring various production options, we settled on nylon powder printing, a technique that captured the flower's ethereal essence perfectly.

The soul of the project, however, lay in an unexpected collaboration with a metalsmith, encountered by chance in a local London market, who crafted the installation's intricate branches. His bemusement at sending metal branches to New York City and complete unfamiliarity with both Alexander McQueen and Saks Fifth Avenue only added to the project's charm.

The installation process involved three very long days and nights of toil behind heavy black curtains. The effort proved well worth it as it culminated in a reveal that stopped famously jaded New Yorkers right in their tracks. The champagne celebration that followed on the rooftop marked not just a successful installation but a further milestone in our journey. Our New York City adventure wasn't finished, however. In true Manhattan fashion, the evening took a dramatic turn when a bomb threat sent us running through the streets, finally finding refuge at our hotel. The juxtaposition of luxury retail and urban chaos perfectly encapsulated the unpredictable nature of creating extraordinary experiences.

This story, from its serendipitous beginnings to its dramatic conclusion, exemplifies our philosophy: true creativity thrives not in spite of challenges but because of them. In the end, it wasn't just about creating beautiful windows; it was about proving that with passion, resourcefulness and determination, even the most ambitious visions can become reality. The Alexander McQueen windows have become more than a successful project for us. They are a testament to the power of creativity and resilience and a reminder that every obstacle represents an opportunity for innovation and the potential for a better solution. In the face of technical challenges, tight deadlines and even urban emergencies, our unwavering commitment to craftsmanship and beauty prevailed. This is the essence of luxury retail design.

We were entrusted by Hermès to design and install the brand's 2016 seasonal windows for their network of airport retail spaces in Paris, London, Munich and Amsterdam. Entitled "Planet Mushroom," this immersive concept brought nature's splendour to life with Hermès' signature storytelling. Each planet represented a unique product category—Men's Ready-to-Wear, Leather Goods, and Women's Ready-to-Wear—blending whimsical humour with refined elegance. The installation was designed to highlight Hermès' unparalleled craftsmanship, inviting visitors on a whimsical journey that celebrated creativity, emotion and the art of luxury.

Paris, London, Munich, Amsterdam Airports / 2016

The Planet Mushroom project for Hermès in 2016 was nothing short of a high-stakes adventure. The sculpted mushrooms and planets initially commissioned by us fell through just one week before they were scheduled to ship to the various destinations, leaving us with a monumental challenge. What followed was a testament to the resilience and resourcefulness of our team. Our production team worked tirelessly aided by extra pairs of hands from Paris, Lyon and the north of England. Even our finance director, friends and family rolled up their sleeves to make it happen. It was an 'all hands on deck' moment during which our team's spirit of determination carried us through.

Rallying together, our team transformed chaos into creation—sourcing and shaping fabrics, embroidering details and ensuring every mushroom, in all their whimsy, met the original specifications approved by the client. Even the constraints of the strictest airport regulations couldn't dampen our spirit. Scenic painting replaced 3D mushrooms where required while adhering to rigorous technical and Health & Safety standards. Against all odds, the windows were installed across multiple countries on time and with breathtaking precision. The result? A magical, humorous and meticulously crafted design concept that celebrated Hermès' storytelling and craftsmanship.

To this day, Planet Mushroom remains one of our most ambitious and beloved projects—a true testament to the power of teamwork and creative problem solving. Looking back at the Planet Mushroom project always brings a smile—it was a daring concept that proves that no matter how bold the idea, flawless execution is everything. But what makes this project truly special is the story behind it. In a moment of crisis, when the odds seemed stacked against us, the L'Atelier Five family came together in an extraordinary show of solidarity. Planet Mushroom remains one of our proudest achievements—a testament to the power of togetherness and the magic of never giving up.

SPECIAL SELECTION AT INTERNATIONAL A' DESIGN AWARD & COMPETITION
BRONZE SELECTION
2018

PENCIL POSSIBILITIES
HERMÈS

In the enchanting world of Hermès, where elegance always marries imagination, even the simplest objects can become the stars of a captivating story. In "Pencil Possibilities," the humble pencil takes centre stage, transforming from a tool of creation into a masterpiece of design. Our mission was to bring this narrative to life across thirty-two windows worldwide, from the bustling boutiques of the United States to the serene stores in Malaysia.

New York, San Francisco, Los Angeles, Honolulu, Vancouver, Kuala Lumpur, Munich / 2017

The challenge was to create a cohesive story that resonated with diverse audiences while highlighting Hermès' iconic elegance. We imagined a series of windows that invited viewers into a journey of creativity, where pencils are not just instruments but storytellers. Each display captured the essence of the design process, showcasing pencils as they sketch garments into existence, their shavings falling gracefully, creating a poetic dance of form and function. Each window was a canvas for innovation, where oversized elements and vibrant hues played together to evoke emotion and inspire imagination. We meticulously 3D modelled each display to fit its unique location, ensuring every detail was tailored to perfection. From the constraints of airport boutiques to standalone stores, our designs seamlessly integrated into each space, transforming it into a stage for our pencil protagonists.

Working with Hermès, we embraced the opportunity to connect with audiences across continents, crafting displays that were as diverse as the locations they inhabited. The pencil, in all its simplicity, became a powerful symbol of creativity and connection, bridging cultures and sparking joy for viewers. As we reflect on “Pencil Possibilities,” we’re reminded of the power of design to transform the ordinary into the extraordinary. Through this project, we celebrated the artistry of Hermès and the timeless charm of the pencil, creating a narrative that invites everyone to pause, reflect and dream.

HERMÈS
HERMÈS

CONNECTED OBJECTS
HERMÈS

We were asked to create a window display that transforms everyday objects into something innovative, playful and profoundly poetic while telling a story that bridges the brand's past and present. To achieve this, our design team devised sleek, subtle designs to echo the characteristic sophistication of Hermès to establish a seamless link between their storied past and their innovative future.

Zurich, Lausanne, Lugano, Basel, Berne / 2017

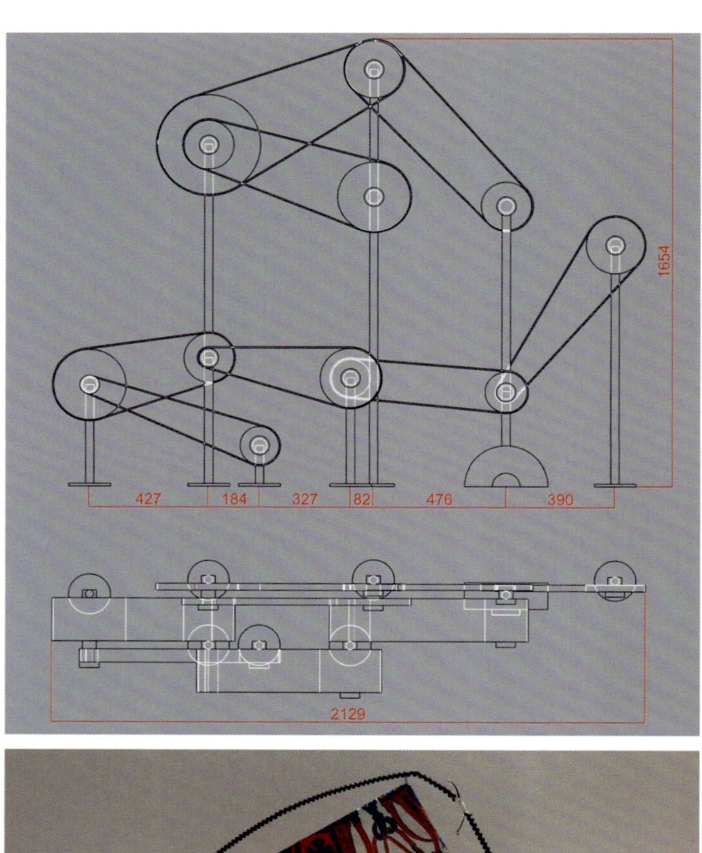

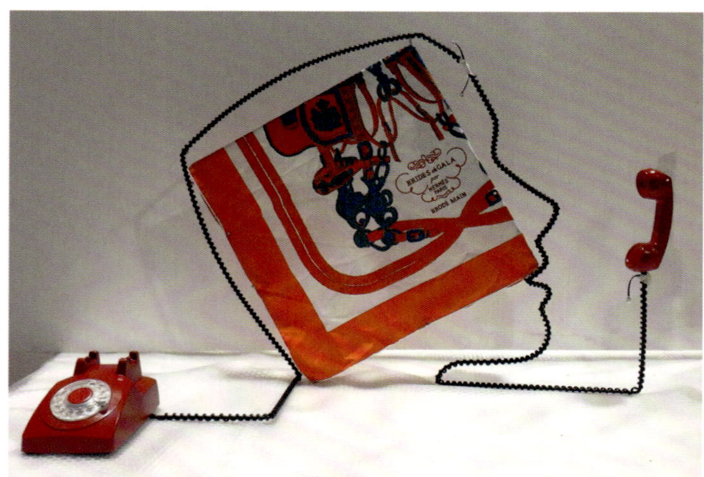

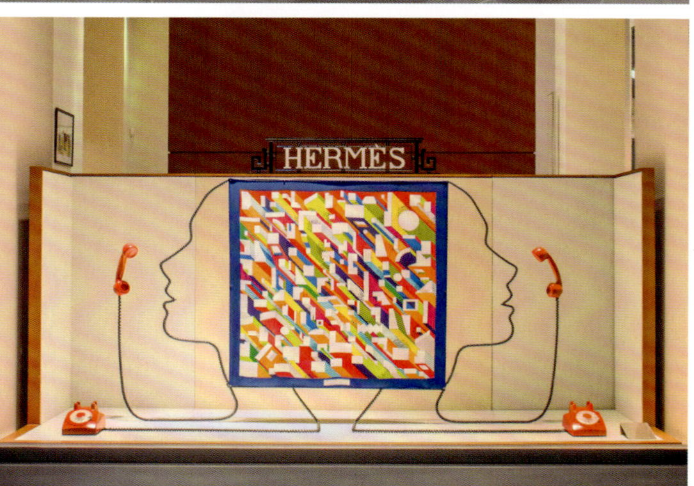

Each piece we crafted was a nod to Hermès' timeless elegance, a tribute to their ability to turn the mundane into the magical. We played with form and function, infusing each object with a narrative that speaks to the soul, a silent conversation between the object and its observer. It's all about connection.

Working with the Hermès team was a joyous exploration of creativity and elegance. Together, we crafted a story that was at once subtle and stunning, a testament to the power of design to evoke emotion and forge connections. It's a beautiful reminder that, in the world of Hermès, every object encapsulates a story, and every design contains a chapter in a much larger narrative.

HERMÈS
HERMÈS
HERMÈS

Züghusplatz
Waaggasse
ausgenommen
HERMÈS
HERMÈS

HANDS MAKE BEAUTY
FENDI

We were asked to create window displays for Fendi's flagship stores in London and Paris that would honour the brand's dedication to artistry and craftsmanship. When Fendi engaged us for this project, we knew this wasn't just about creating store window displays. It was about celebrating the poetry of the human hand and its role in perpetuating centuries of tradition involved in crafting the house's luxurious products.

Sloane Street & Bond Street, London, and Rue St Honoré, Paris / 2017

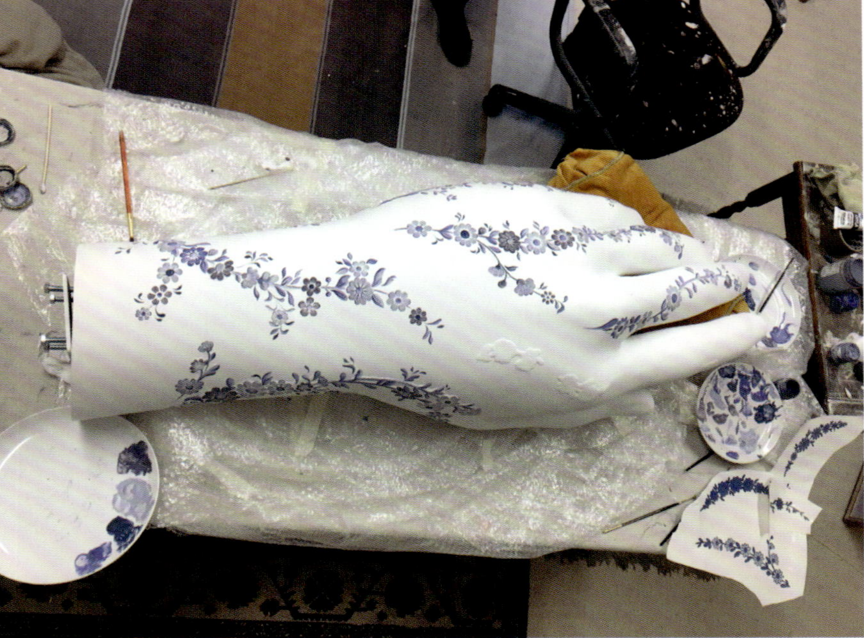

The challenge was to find a way to capture the poetry of movement involved in the human hand in a static display while remaining faithful to the brand's characteristic elegance. How do you make a pair of hands tell the story of Fendi's craftsmanship in a way that is culturally relevant but without being, well, heavy-handed? We finally settled on large-scale sculptures featuring a pair of human hands forming various gestures including the 'heart hands gesture,' a universal symbol of love and unity in the lexicon of visual communication and a nod to Gen Z's favourite social media signature. Our wonderful team of sculptors and painters set about the task of crafting these hand sculptures that would eventually grace the windows of Fendi's flagship stores in London and Paris. The project took on a more personal note when we discovered that our project manager's mother, a flower artist whose brushes have danced across canvases for more than twenty-five years, had a true gift for painting delicate blooms. Who better to add that final touch of whimsy to our heart hands sculpture than someone whose own hands had spent a quarter-century bringing flowers to life?

Working alongside Fendi's design team was like being part of a beautiful duet. They trusted our vision and we honoured their legacy of artisanal excellence. Together, we created something that was more than a window display. It became a story told through sculpture, form and shadow, celebrating the hands that craft luxury and the eyes that appreciate it. The result? Windows that stop people in their tracks, forcing them to take a few fleeting moments from their hectic day to appreciate the beauty of human artistry and its crucial role in crafting luxury.

"Saina cares deeply about the work but also for the people around her. She genuinely wants people to succeed and that in turn makes you want to work harder. It's a reflection of who she is."

Luke Mills, Studio Manager, L'Atelier Five

ROLLERCOASTER
BUCHERER

We were tasked with crafting an entertaining display tailored to draw visitors to Selfridges' Wonder Room in order to celebrate the launch of Bucherer's sixteen Blue Edition watches. In the heart of bustling Selfridges, where the world of luxury watches meets the vibrant energy of a shopping heaven, we crafted a spectacle that captured the imagination and celebrates the delight of these unique watches.

Selfridges' Wonder Room, London / 2017

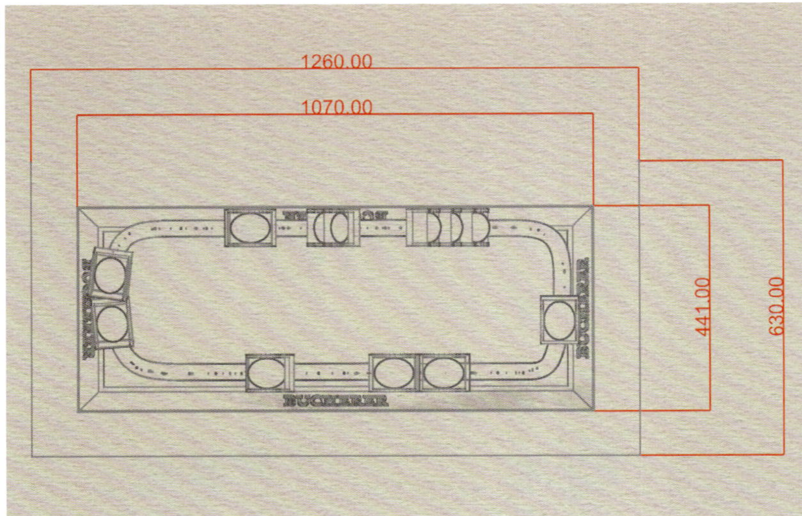

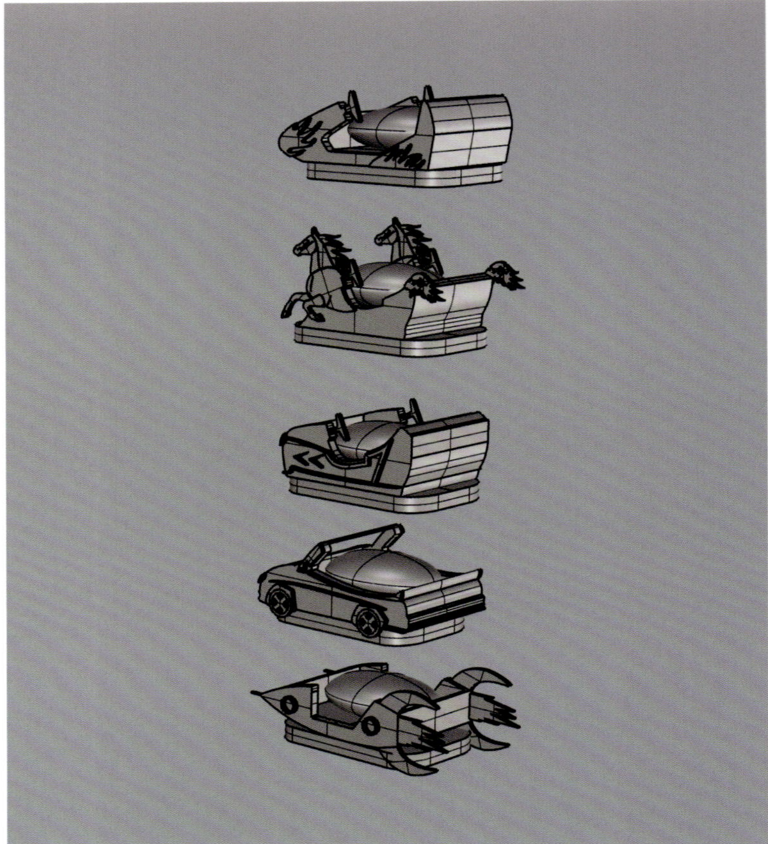

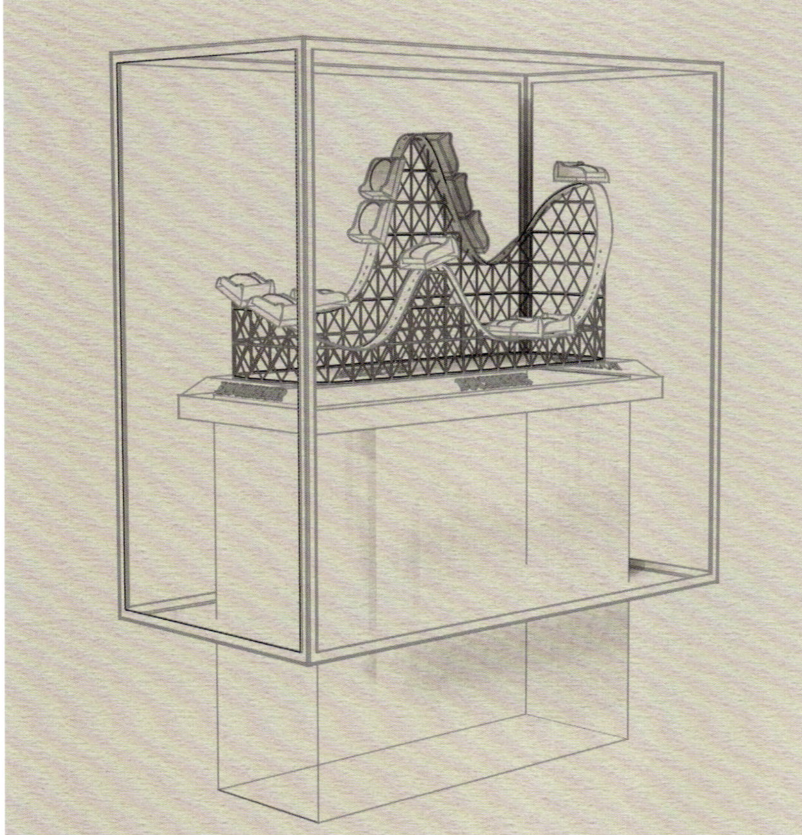

For this project, our challenge was how to capture the imagination of the shoppers and provide a delightful visual story worthy of the launch of the sixteen Blue Edition watches. Enter the magic of LED chasing lights, a brilliant solution that brought this miniature amusement park with its bespoke rollercoaster carriages to life. The lights created a mesmerising effect of movement, drawing eyes and sparking curiosity from every angle. It's a testament to our commitment to marrying creativity with practicality, ensuring that each design was not only visually stunning but also commercially savvy. The flexibility of the design allowed for carriages to be removed as each watch finds its new owner, a thoughtful touch that speaks to our understanding of retail dynamics. It's this blend of artistry and functionality that makes the Bucherer Blue Edition display a true masterpiece. As you stand before this captivating scene, you're not just looking at watches; you're experiencing a story, a celebration of craftsmanship and innovation. Each watch tells a tale of precision and elegance, and together, they form a narrative that is as dynamic as the world around them.

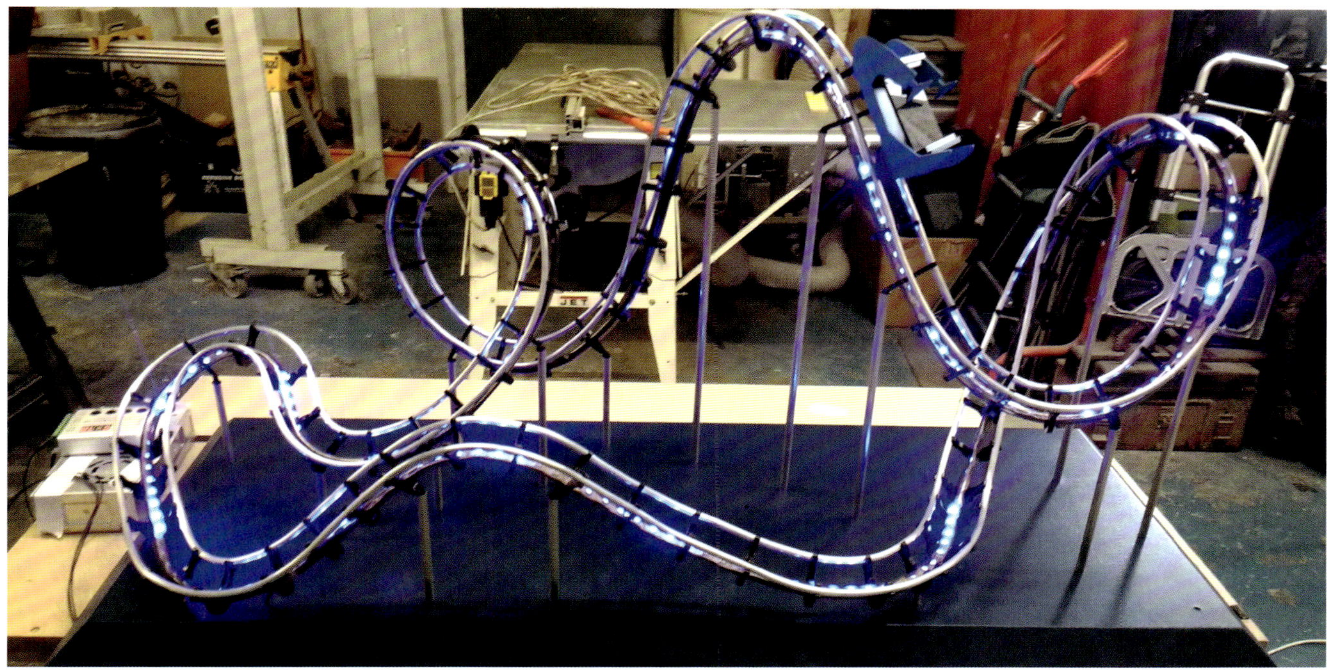

This wasn't just a display; it was a journey, a playful dance of light and motion that invited every passerby to pause and marvel. Picture this: a 360-degree window, in the shape of a tank, where sixteen bespoke carriages glide gracefully, each one cradling a limited-edition watch. It's a rollercoaster of elegance, where the watches are the stars, each carriage a stage for their unique beauty. The challenge was to create something that not only captivated but also adapted to the dynamic environment of a busy shopping floor. In this collaboration with Bucherer, we created more than a display; we crafted an experience, a moment of wonder in the everyday hustle of life. It's a reminder that luxury is not just about the product but the journey it takes you on, the emotions it evokes and the memories it creates.

BUCHERE
BUCHERE
Exit to Oxford Street
BUC

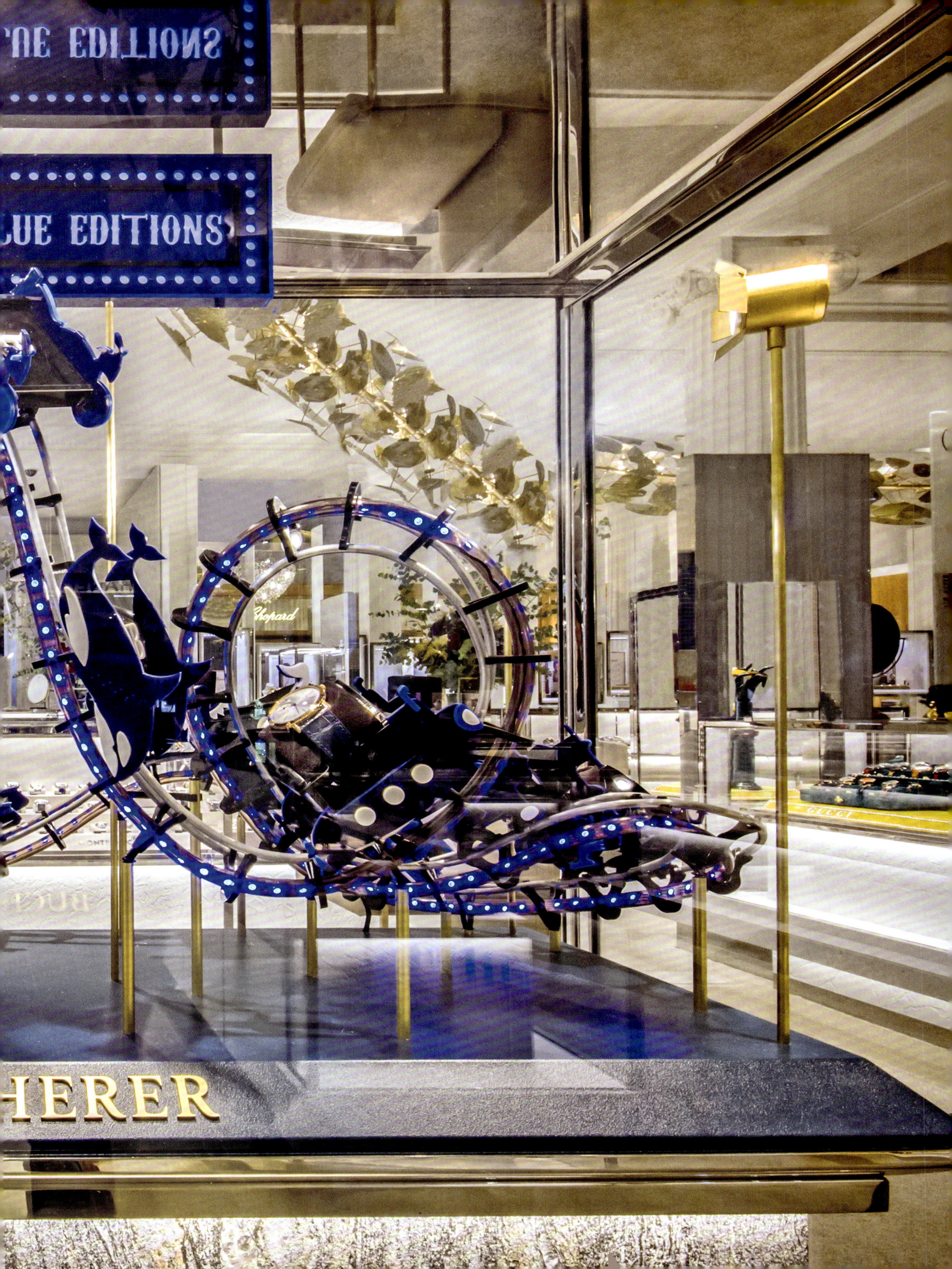
LUE EDITIONS
Chopard
HERER

CINDERELLA
PATEK PHILIPPE

We were asked to create a series of eight whimsical window displays that would invite busy passers-by to pause, dream and discover the artistry of Patek Philippe through a fresh lens.

London, Paris, Geneva / 2017

Working closely with Patek Philippe's creative artistic director, we drew inspiration from the classic fairytale "Cinderella" to create a compelling narrative around time and the stroke of midnight. Our modern-day Cinderella story doesn't begin with a glass slipper, but rather with a masterpiece of horology taking centre stage. Like chapters in a beloved storybook, eight enchanting windows unfold across London, Paris and Geneva, each one more captivating than the last.

Combining traditional craftsmanship with contemporary design techniques, our artisans hand-sculpted everything from graceful carriages to our mischievous mouse friend who guides viewers through the story, while silk prints shimmer like starlight against carefully crafted backgrounds. We created a world where 2D and 3D elements waltzed together, bringing to life the storied salons of Patek Philippe from Paris to London and Geneva.

"'Giving up' is not part of Saina's vocabulary."

Kris Sparks, Finance Director, L'Atelier Five

While the narrative grew out of a fairytale, the installation phase of this project was less than enchanting. We were on a particularly tight deadline, grappling to install tricky window vinyls and starting to run out of both time and steam. Saina Attaoui, our founder and managing director, stepped out to pick up sustenance at a nearby supermarket when she noticed two vinyl installers finishing up for the day. After explaining our predicament, she persuaded them to come lend a hand. Thanks to a conversation, serendipity and the kindness of two random strangers, our windows were transformed just in time, proving that sometimes the best partnerships begin with a simple hello over the bread aisle.

2018
RUSSIA
HUBLOT LOVES FOOTBALL
SPECIAL SELECTION AT INTERNATIONAL A' DESIGN AWARD & COMPETITION
BRONZE SELECTION
2019

FIFA 2018—HUBLOT LOVES FOOTBALL
HUBLOT

When the marketing director of Hublot approached us with the challenge of bringing the excitement of the World Cup into the luxurious halls of Harrods, we embarked on a journey that would blend the worlds of sport and luxury in a way that had never been done before. Our task was clear: to create an installation that not only celebrated football but also resonated with the elegance and sophistication of one of the world's most prestigious department stores.

Harrods, London / 2018

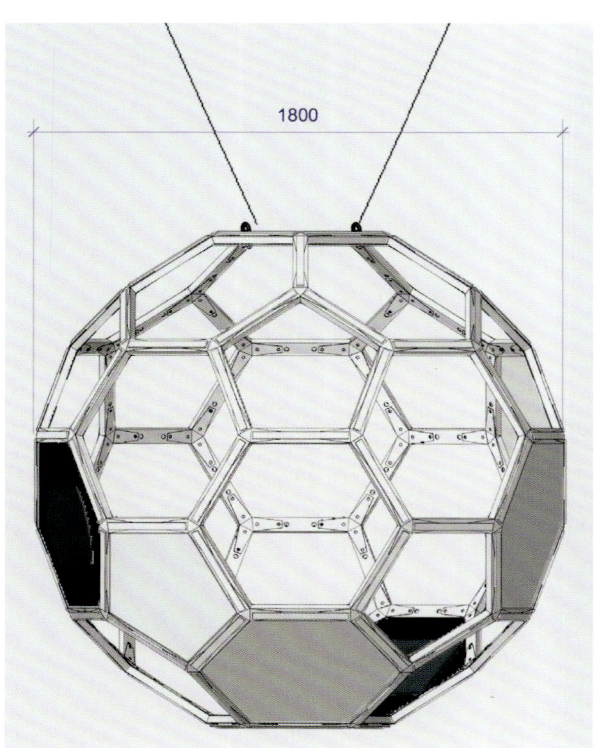

The concept was as ambitious as it was thrilling. Imagine walking into Harrods and being greeted by three giant, multifaceted footballs suspended above, each one a vibrant beacon of the World Cup spirit. These weren't just any footballs; they were technological marvels, equipped with digital screens to display live scores, countdowns and even the sound of a whistle echoing through the atrium when a goal was scored. It was a celebration of Hublot's role as the Official Timekeeper of the World Cup, a position that speaks to precision, excellence and global connection.

But this project was more than just a visual spectacle. It was an interactive experience that brought the thrill of the games to life. The challenge was to maintain a delicate balance between the dynamic energy of the World Cup and the refined atmosphere of Harrods. Our design seamlessly integrated the football campaign across six windows, an interactive atrium installation and engaging pop-up spaces within Harrods and Watches of Switzerland. It was a powerful demonstration of our commitment to creating experiences that are impactful, engaging and commercially savvy.

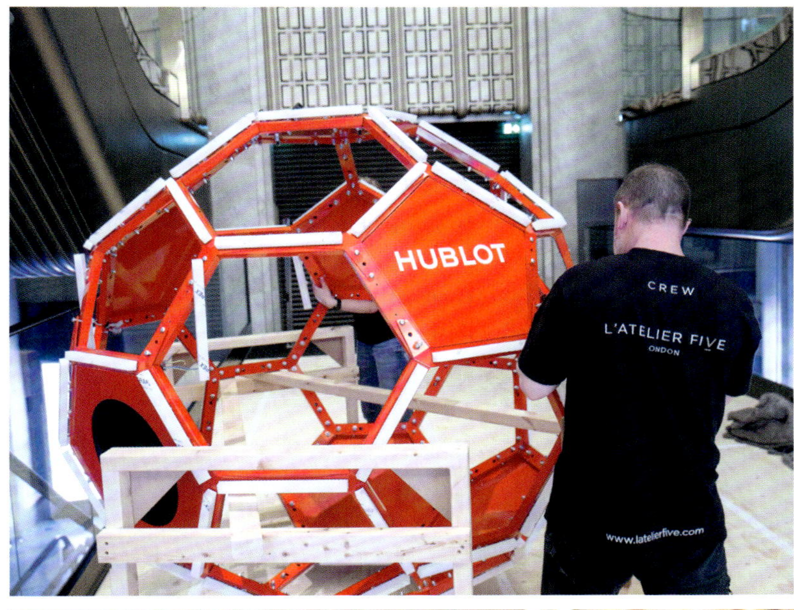

HUBLOT
CREW
L'ATELIER FIVE
www.latelierfive.com
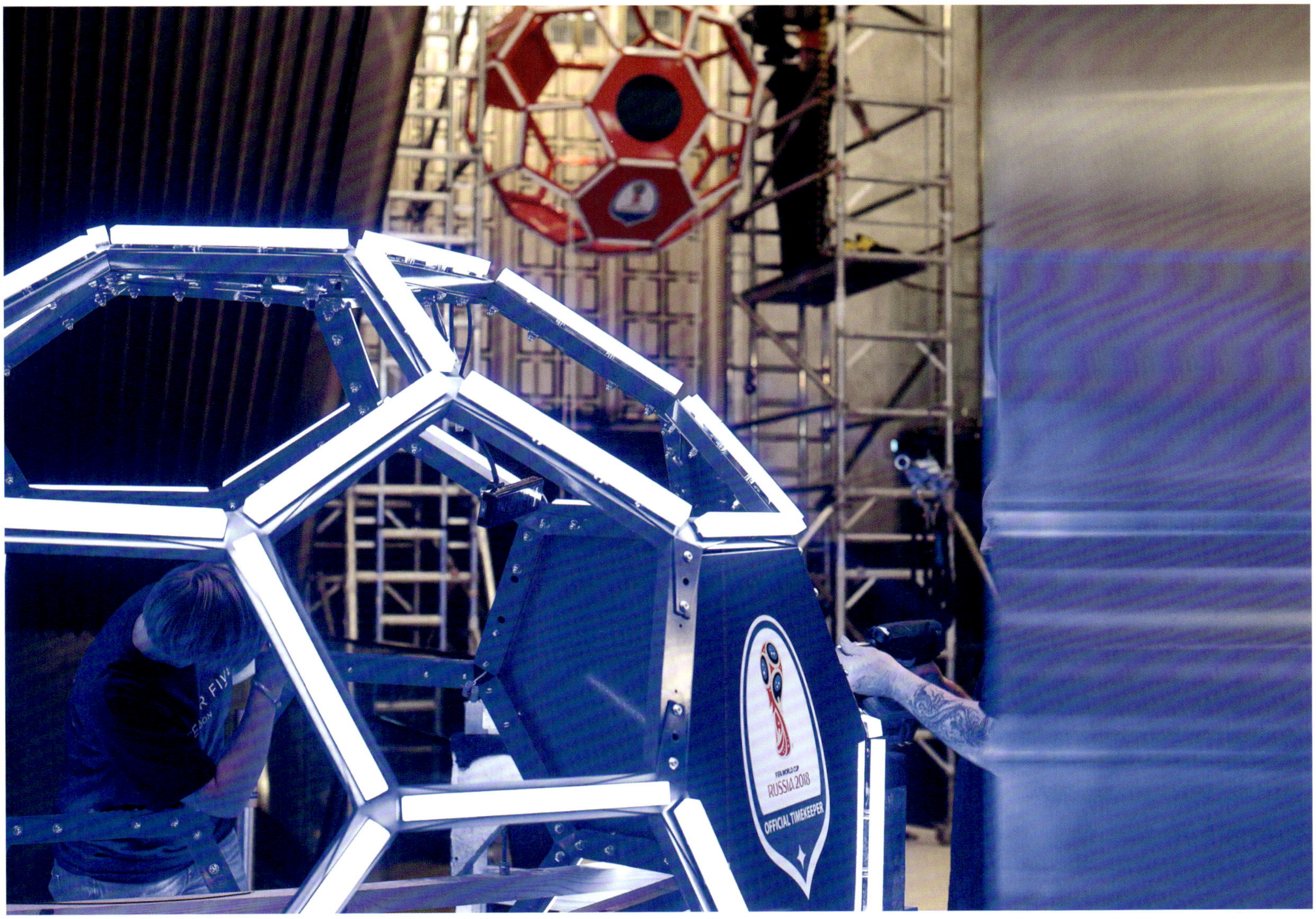
RUSSIA 2018
OFFICIAL TIMEKEEPER

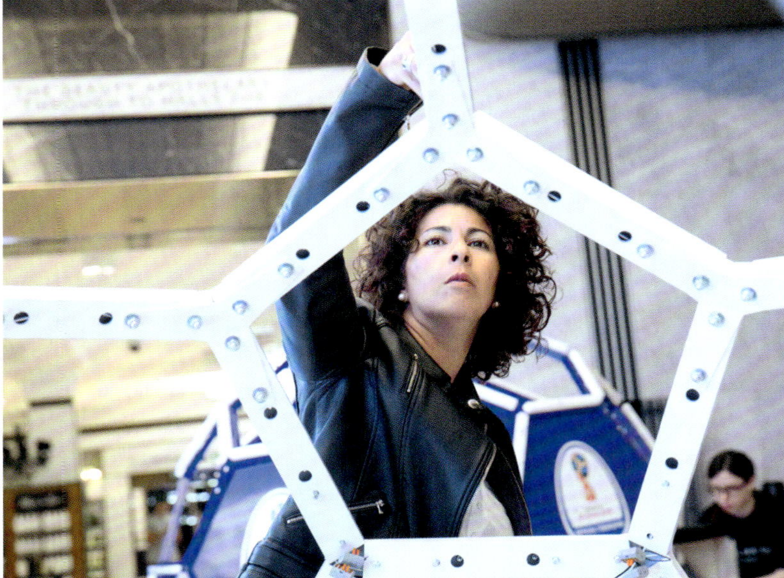

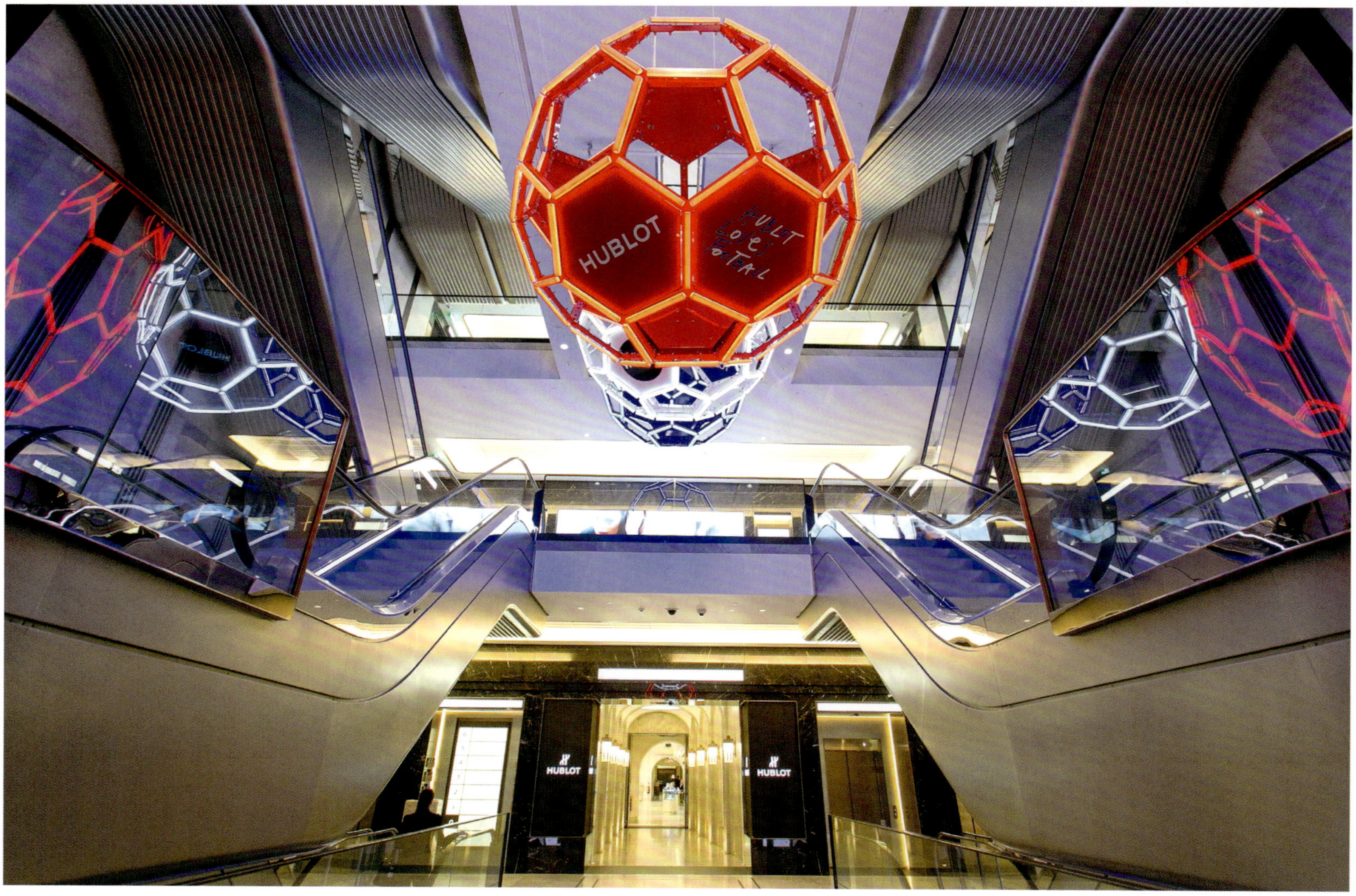

This project was not just about celebrating a sporting event: it was about connecting people through a shared passion, transcending cultural and geographical boundaries. It was a reminder that in a world of diverse interests, there are moments that unite us all. And for this innovative fusion of sport and luxury, we were honoured with an A'Design Award in 2019, a recognition of our dedication to excellence.

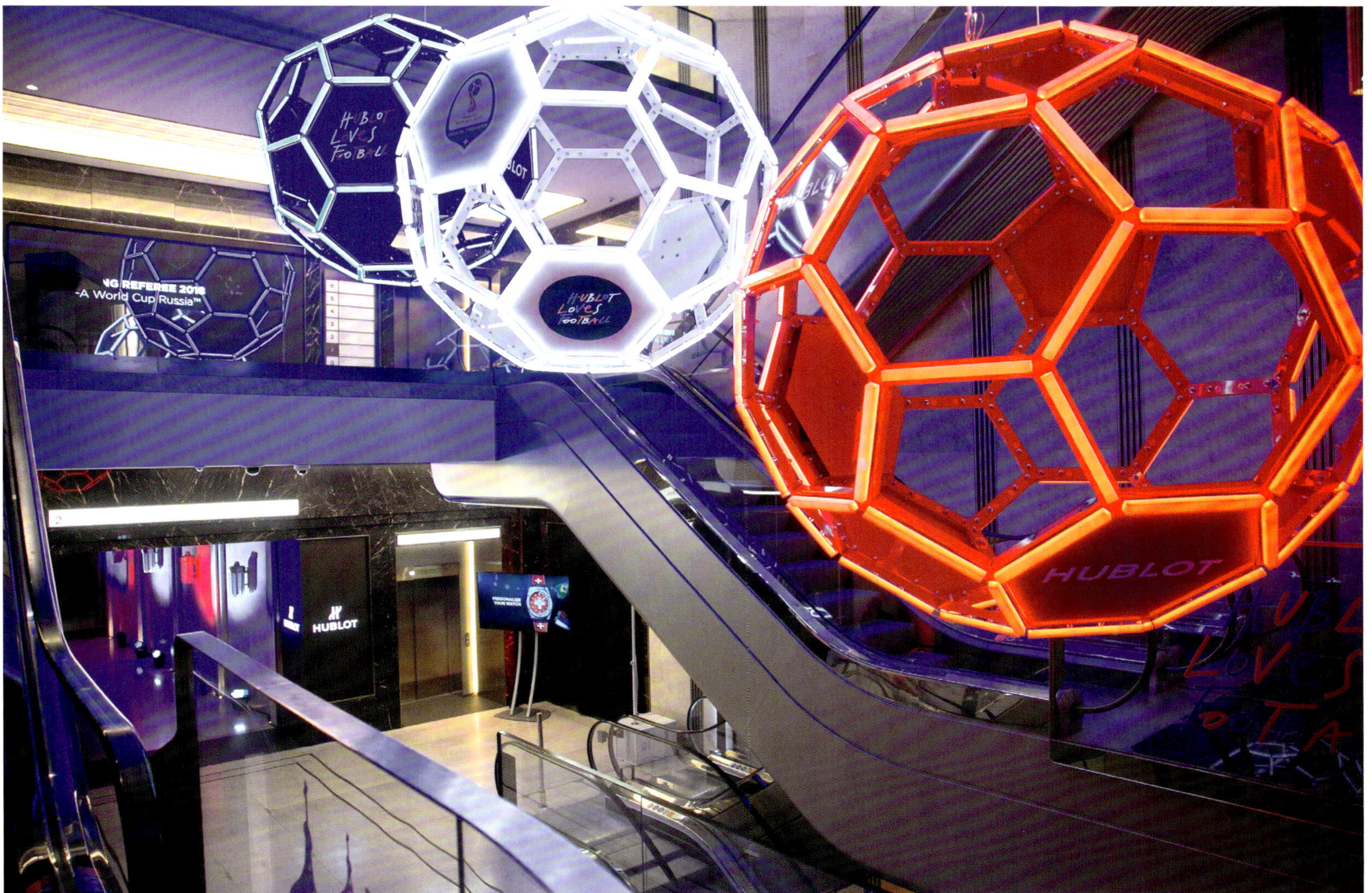

As we reflect on this journey, we're reminded of the power of design to bring people together, to create moments of joy and connection and to celebrate the beauty of collaboration. In partnership with Hublot, we created more than an installation; we crafted a memory, a moment in time that will be cherished by all who experienced it.

HUBLOT
LOVES
FOOTBALL

HUBLOT
HUBLOT
LOVES
FOTBALL
HUBLOT
HUBLOT

ure an
y" –
iming

THE MASTER COLLECTION AND THE 1,000 HOURS CONTROL

In 1992, the new Master Collection inaugurates the 1,000 Hours Control, a quality check programme which now subjects finished watches to a battery of rigorous tests covering every aspect of performance of all watches produced by the Manufacture.

2007

DUOMÈTRE AND DUAL WING® CONCEPT

Inspired by an 1880 chronometer, the Dual-Wing concept invented by Jaeger-LeCoultre is revolutionary in two ways, as dual, yet independent, mechanisms united by a single regulating organ provide the Duomètre collection with guaranteed performance ...d precision.

185TH ANNIVERSARY EXHIBITION
JAEGER-LECOULTRE

Jaeger-LeCoultre's takeover of the windows and pop-up area on Brompton Road at Harrods was a spectacular celebration of their 185 years of heritage and innovation. This event marked the unveiling of their new Polaris collection and a brand-new Jaeger-LeCoultre boutique. Working alongside their talented team, we brought their rich heritage and vision to life, featuring original models from the 1960s. This offered a nostalgic nod to the brand's storied past while highlighting their continued commitment to craftsmanship and excellence. It was a fitting tribute to Jaeger-LeCoultre's enduring legacy in the world of luxury timepieces.

Harrods, London / 2018

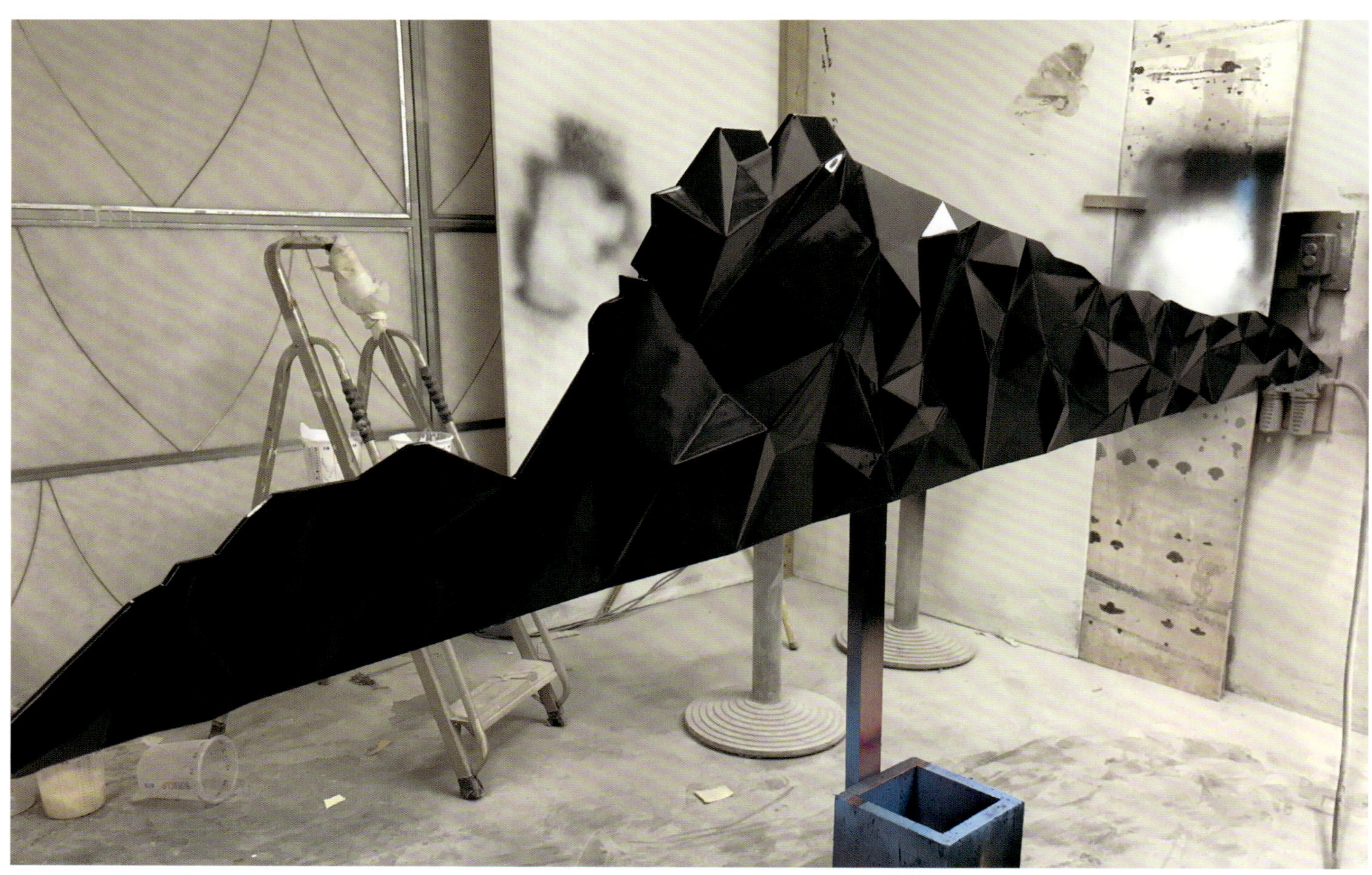

BORN IN 1833 IN THE VALLÉE DE JOUX, NESTLED IN THE SWISS JURA MOUNTAINS
1900
1920
LECOULTRE MEETS JAEGER
In 1903, Paris-based watchmaker to the French Navy, Edmond Jaeger, challenges Swiss manufacturers to develop and produce the ultra-thin movements that he has invented. Jacques-David LeCoultre, Antoine's grandson who is responsible for production at LeCoultre & Cie., accepts the challenge.
THE ATMOS PATENT
In 1928, Jean-Léon Reutter develops the first clock with a semi-perpetual movement enabling the mechanism to wind itself. Reutter sells the Atmos patent to LeCoultre on July 27th 1935 and the technique, redesigned and improved by Jaeger-LeCoultre, endures today.
1929
CALIBRE 101
1950
MEMOVOX
1990
2000
THE MASTER COLLECTION AND THE 1,000 HOURS CONTROL
2012

The project also involved the intricate use of stone finishes and CNC (computer numerical control) detailing, further enhancing the luxurious feel and precision that Jaeger-LeCoultre is celebrated for. These elements were carefully integrated alongside high-quality materials like oak, wood and chalk panels, creating a cohesive and sophisticated design. Our team's expertise was crucial in bringing all these components together seamlessly, ensuring that every detail met Health & Safety regulations and stayed within budget, all in a tight timeline. This reflects our dedication to craftsmanship, innovation and the art of creating unforgettable retail experiences.

This project truly stands as a masterpiece, executed with exceptional attention to detail and production engineering. It's a testament to our commitment to excellence and precision, and we couldn't be prouder of the outcome. Every element came together beautifully, showcasing the dedication and skill of our team in creating an unforgettable retail experience.

"Saina is unwavering in the face of adversity. No matter how big the problem that presents itself, her attitude is always 'there's a solution and we will find it.'"

Sophie Quilling, Operations Manager 2016–2018, L'Atelier Five

JAEGER-LECOULTRE

OBLIQUE PATTERN
DIOR

Our brief was crystal clear: to help launch the iconic Dior tote bag by translating Dior's vision into an engaging pop-up space at Harrods. Shoppers were introduced to this timeless bag for the very first time, and the pop-up celebrated the icon by being fully adorned with the actual fabric featuring Dior's oblique logos. These logos were in colours that represented the first collection, making the experience both a tribute to Dior's legacy and a captivating introduction to its future.

Harrods, London / 2018

Our technical challenge was immense, as we used the actual Dior fabric, which required special treatment to meet fire prevention standards in accordance with Health & Safety regulations and Harrods' guidelines. Once treated, this fabric became quite difficult to manipulate. The entire pop-up was enveloped in this fabric, demanding precision in aligning each oblique and ensuring a smooth, seamless application. Our incredibly skilled team rose to the occasion, achieving this with finesse. The memory of working with this fabric remains vivid, a strong reminder of our dedication to detail and excellence.

Our inaugural pop-up with Dior was nothing short of extraordinary, marking the launch of the legendary Dior Book Tote. Inspired by a drawing from the 1967 Dior archives, this pop-up celebrated the tote bag's heritage and personalisation. Shoppers were treated to a full personalisation ceremony, immersing them in the artistry and elegance that Dior embodies. It was a unique opportunity to bring a piece of fashion history to life, creating an unforgettable experience for every visitor.

CHRISTIAN DIOR
CHRISTIAN DIOR

HARRODS
Harrods
Harrods
ROGER DUBUIS
ROGER DUBUIS
PERTAMINA

ROGER DUBUIS X LAMBORGHINI SQUADRA CORSE
ROGER DUBUIS

Our mission for this project was to craft an innovative and engaging pop-up to celebrate the luxury watch brand Roger Dubuis and its exciting new collaboration with Lamborghini Squadra Corse. This summer pop-up event at Harrods was a testament to the synergy between high-performance engineering and exquisite watchmaking. Working closely with their HQ team, we were dedicated to translating their vision while honouring the engineering prowess that Lamborghini represents, alongside the meticulous watchmaking processes and materials of Roger Dubuis. The centrepiece of this event is the stunning Excalibur Aventador S, a masterpiece created in collaboration with Lamborghini Squadra Corse and limited to just eighty-eight pieces worldwide.

Harrods, London / 2018

Our technical challenge was a thrilling endeavour, seamlessly merging the intricate craftsmanship of Roger Dubuis watches with the C-SMC carbon of Lamborghini's supercars. The watches, driven by an 'engine' inspired by the Aventador, were showcased in a captivating display. We used a programmed chasing light that started from one window, where the Lamborghini was on display, and led to the next, engaging passers-by and inviting them to immerse themselves in the full Roger Dubuis experience. This pop-up offered a discovery of the complex, engineered world of racing cars and watchmaking. Transporting the Lamborghini, a giant piece of art, into the space was a challenge we relished and completed without a hitch. This unique pop-up execution perfectly reflected the spirit and innovation of both Lamborghini and Roger Dubuis, creating an unforgettable experience for all who visited.

It was truly an incredible experience collaborating with the Roger Dubuis team, especially in crafting such an intricately engineered pop-up. The technical demands and expertise required for these projects are immense, and it's clear that our team rose to the occasion beautifully. It's always a bit bittersweet to see such a masterpiece come to an end after a short time, but the impact and unique execution leave a lasting impression, embodying the signature essence of the Roger Dubuis universe.

Harrods
ROGER DUBU
EXCALIBUR

HARRODS Ltd
Harrods
PERTAMINA
63

Download Your
CLASH DE Cartier
Playlist By Michel Gaubert
DUKE STREET W1
creative retail awards
WINNER
2021

CLASH DE CARTIER
CARTIER

We were tasked by Cartier UK to design a month-long pop-up event for the launch of the new Cartier jewel ery, "Clash de Cartier." Scheduled for the month of August when The Corner Shop at Selfridges sees a surge of international travellers, we were asked to design an event that would appeal to both international and local clients involving a blend of experiential and commercial elements with a strong focus on appealing to millennials.

Selfridges, London / 2019

Watch the video

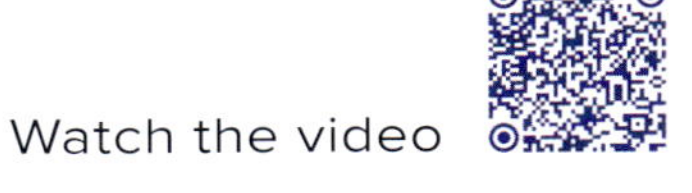

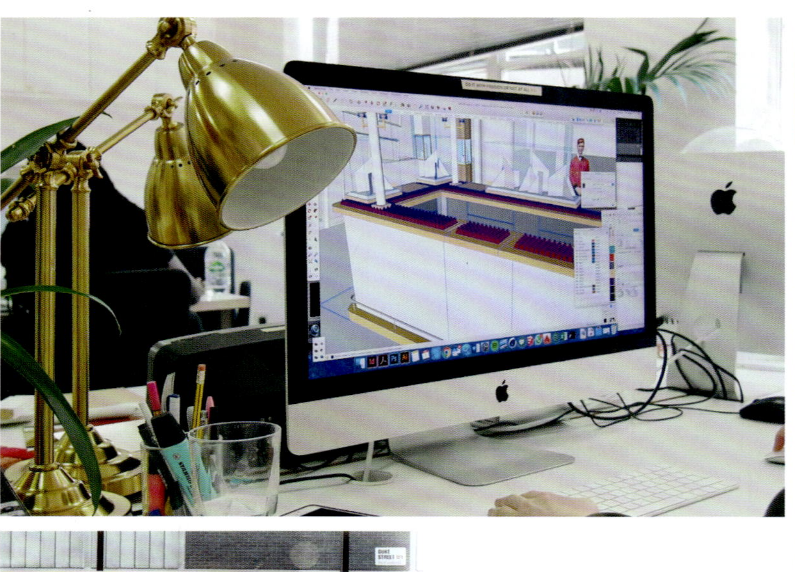

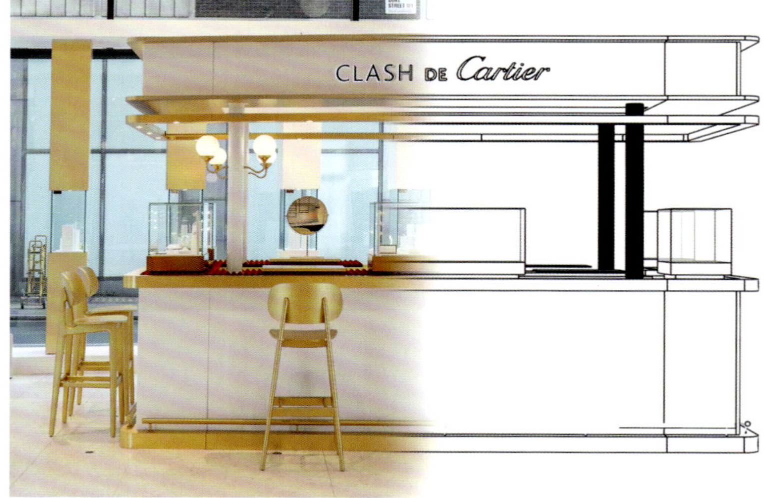

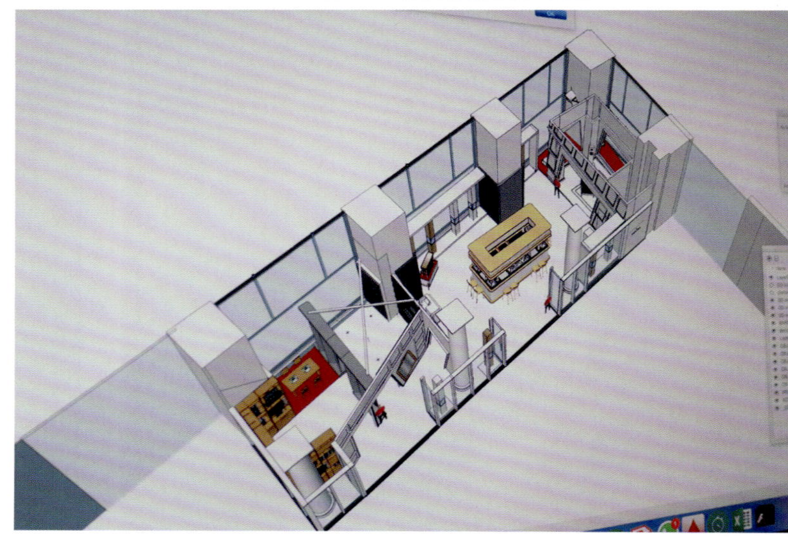

The technical challenges of this project involved ensuring that multiple touchpoints seamlessly came together to create an engaging and smooth journey for shoppers. Our goal was to make everyone who entered the space fall in love with the collection just as we had. We divided the space into distinct experiences including an immersion into the "Clash" world; interactive encounters; digital personalisation; selling experience; and opportunities for sharing and keeping memories. We developed a full 360-degree event that included experiential touchpoints such as the Clash de Cartier personality test, touch-and-try Clash de Cartier bar, captivating photo moments and live haiku poem sessions.

A typical challenge in this type of project is adhering to the venue's Health & Safety guidelines. Add to that recruitment of a team of bell boys, several professional photographers and haiku poets on-site, all of whom needed to be present throughout the store's opening hours for the entire month. We assembled a fantastic team to manage this activation, ensuring everyone was properly briefed to represent the values and ethics of the Cartier brand.

CLASH DE Cartier
NIGHTCLUB
CHATEAU
CLASH
DE
Cartier

"What I love about our team is that everyone comes from different places. Interacting closely with people from different cultures and different backgrounds has a direct impact on how we approach a project. It allows us to collaborate more effectively and to come up with truly unique concepts."

Anya Tunjic, Designer, L'Atelier Five

This project was truly a story of love, laughter and hard work. The bonds we formed and the experiences we shared made it an unforgettable journey. From the fully immersive activation to the incredible teamwork, every moment was filled with passion and dedication. Launching the pop-up on our managing director Saina's birthday, followed by the Dior opening, felt like a celebration of everything we had accomplished together. As a personal milestone, Saina treated herself to a ring from the collection, a reminder of the love and effort we poured into this project. It marked a significant chapter in our journey, leading to the opening of our office in Dubai. For this, we will always be grateful. Our long-term friendship with Cartier is a testament to the love and laughter that fuelled our hard work, and we wouldn't have it any other way.

CLASH DE Cartier
CORNER SHOP

OXFORD
STREET W1
CITY OF WESTMINSTER
SELFRIDGE
& Co
LIMITED

DIOR
CHRISTIAN DIOR
CHRISTIAN DIOR

CHECK-IN DIOR
DIOR

For the launch of Dior's Fall–Winter 2019–2020 Ready-to-Wear collection by Maria Grazia Chiuri, we were thrilled to be entrusted with a pop-up project that resonated deeply with our French roots and London base. This brief was perfect for us, as it allowed us to bring Dior's vision to life in a vibrant and culturally rich setting. The collection featured a selection of ready-to-wear, footwear and bags, including the Dior Book Tote, unveilec in an exclusive version adorned with the Union Jack motif. Their unique ABCDior personalisation service offered shoppers the chance to customise their pieces, adding a personal touch to their luxury experience. The pop-up store's colour scheme mirrored the show's palette, with variations of black combined with green, red or white checks, celebrating British culture. The homage extended to iconic British symbols like a telephone booth and an English taxi, all clad in the same motifs.

Harrods, London / 2019

The technical challenge for this project was to ensure that every bespoke element matched the collection's colours so perfectly that it acted like a chameleon, unveiling itself to the shopper when they enter the pop-up. The wrapping of the checks in the Dior pattern had to be flawlessly applied and aligned, reflecting Dior's unwavering attention to detail and craftsmanship. Each execution challenged us to push our talents and expertise to meet the perfection embodied by the Dior brand. The result, as always, was spectacular and rewarding, especially when working with a temporary installation. Adding a wrapped vintage black taxi to the Harrods window was a fun and creative touch that brought the entire experience to life.

DIOR
CHRISTIAN DIOR
DIOR

For the second year in a row, it's become a cherished tradition to celebrate Saina's birthday with the Dior team while we're working overnight on an installation. There's something incredibly special about sharing these moments with such a talented group, and the result of our hard work—the satisfaction of a captivated audience—is truly the best gift she could ask for. It's a perfect blend of celebration and creativity that makes her birthday unforgettable every time.

"At L'Atelier Five, not only is everybody accepted but they are celebrated. There really couldn't be a more inclusive place to work."

Luke Mills, Studio Manager, L'Atelier Five

DIOR
CHRISTIAN DIOR

CHRISTIAN DIOR
CHRISTIAN DIOR
AFFÈ

200TH ANNIVERSARY BURLINGTON CHRISTMAS
BURLINGTON ARCADE

We were truly honoured to have been commissioned to design the concept for the iconic Burlington Arcade for the celebration of its 200th anniversary since being built by Lord George Cavendish for Lady Cavendish. We were tasked with bringing to life the rich stories of the past two centuries through immersive installations, personalisation, bespoke services and experiences. We opted for a beautiful snowy blizzard beneath the arches with skylights in the iconic landmark creating a soft and moving art-like installation that captured the spirit of the festive season and the momentous celebration of Burlington Arcade's 200th anniversary.

Burlington Arcade, London / 2019

Watch the video

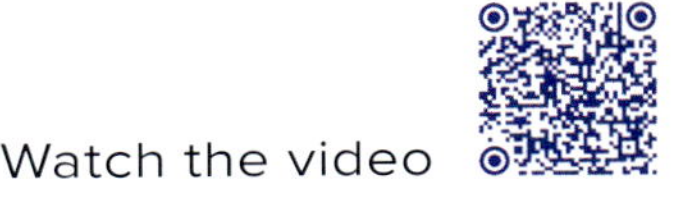

We needed to ensure the installation was elevated above the foot traffic so as not to impede the circulation of customers and passers-by. It was also very important for us to ensure the design complemented the building's beautiful architecture. The goal was to create an immersive art-like installation cascading from the high ceilings and enveloping visitors in a winter wonderland. Finally, we also wanted to reference Burlington Arcade's rich past so chose a gold, white and red colour palette referencing the iconic beadle's uniforms, which really bought a sense of continuity to the overall look and feel.

We used 350 metres of handcrafted gold ribbon and ran it the entire length of the arcade along with more than 12,000 handcrafted abstract paper snowflakes, using a scoring method that gave the paper movement in the wind. The snowflakes were entwined with 240 twinkling fairy lights to create that extra bit of Christmas magic as customers walked through the immersive installation. The lights reflected the pearlised paper used for this installation to replicate the effect of real snow, creating depth and interest throughout. The installation required three months of toil by more than eighty dedicated team members—including designers, project managers, production teams and paper artists—and three long nights to install.

Burlington Arcade was an amazing project to work on. It combined heritage, artistry, lighting and an immersive experience. We really wanted to showcase this as a Christmas destination for people to experience the Arcade as they never had before, highlighting its British heritage through the architectural arches. We wanted to create an installation that would entice passers-by into the Arcade so they could be immersed in a unique shopping experience, creating a memory of that moment. We also had the privilege of being part of Burlington Arcade's launch night. Our team coordinated with the Burlington Arcade events team to ensure the lights were switched on when their special guest, Dame Judi Dench, pulled the switch.

BAUDOIN & LANGE

ABC
DI
OR
CD
PERSONALIZATION AVAILABLE
CHRISTIAN DIOR
PARIS

NEON FLOCK
DIOR

For the launch of the Autumn–Winter 2020–2021 Ready-to-Wear collection, Dior tasked us to create an immersive velvet pop-up space at Harrods, referencing the brand's use of the luscious fabric throughout the collection. This project was all about emphasising the delicate softness of velvet in vibrant, autumnal shades that beautifully represented their collection. The luxurious texture and rich colours of the velvet provided a sensuous experience perfectly capturing the essence of Dior's elegant and sophisticated design.

Harrods, London / 2020

The challenge of this project lay in part in the need to harmonise materials in the same Pantone colours while accommodating different textures and varied application. Meticulous planning and execution was required in order to create a seamless integration of colour, textures and materials. Our use of flocking techniques on furniture and walls added a satin finish, enhancing the tactile experience and reflecting the softness of the collection. This finish invited people to caress the surfaces thereby evoking the softness and elegance of the collection. It was tangible evidence of our attention to detail and ability to create a cohesive and immersive environment that resonated with Dior's vision.

The shopping space was a true visual delight, exuding a sense of beauty and romantic allure. The pastel colour-blocking was executed with precision, creating an ambience that was both comforting and inviting. The warm and cosy atmosphere enveloped visitors, making them feel at ease while exploring the collection. What made this space even more impressive was the technical mastery behind it. Understanding the technical intricacies behind the scenes only deepens one's appreciation for the work. It's a testament to the skill, creativity and attention to detail that went into crafting such a remarkable space. This project not only showcased our ability to create visually stunning environments but also highlighted the depth of expertise required to achieve such a harmonious and immersive experience.

CHRIST

AN DIOR

ID SBID INTERNATIONAL DESIGN 2022 AWARDS
WINNER

PANTHÈRE DE CARTIER—LONDON
CARTIER

The brief was to create an interactive luxury experience in Harrods' exhibition windows celebrating the story and heritage of Panthère de Cartier through a series of experiential rooms and playful takeaways. Internal Cartier guidelines drove the initial storytelling and were then elevated to create an immersive experience in true L'Atelier Five style. Our goal was to push the boundaries to show our client a modern, impactful pop-up. The central idea was to provide a 360-degree experience so that the visitor could take home a piece of the pop-up as a memorable takeaway either via a branded giveaway or a bespoke photo moment. Our team created a digital tunnel with state-of-the-art AV equipment featuring digital content developed around the Panthère history and iconic creations, including a sleek touch-and-try area where visitors were invited to interact with the collection and take a memorable selfie in the faceted mirror. Our aim, as always, was to engage and enchant visitors.

Harrods, London / 2020

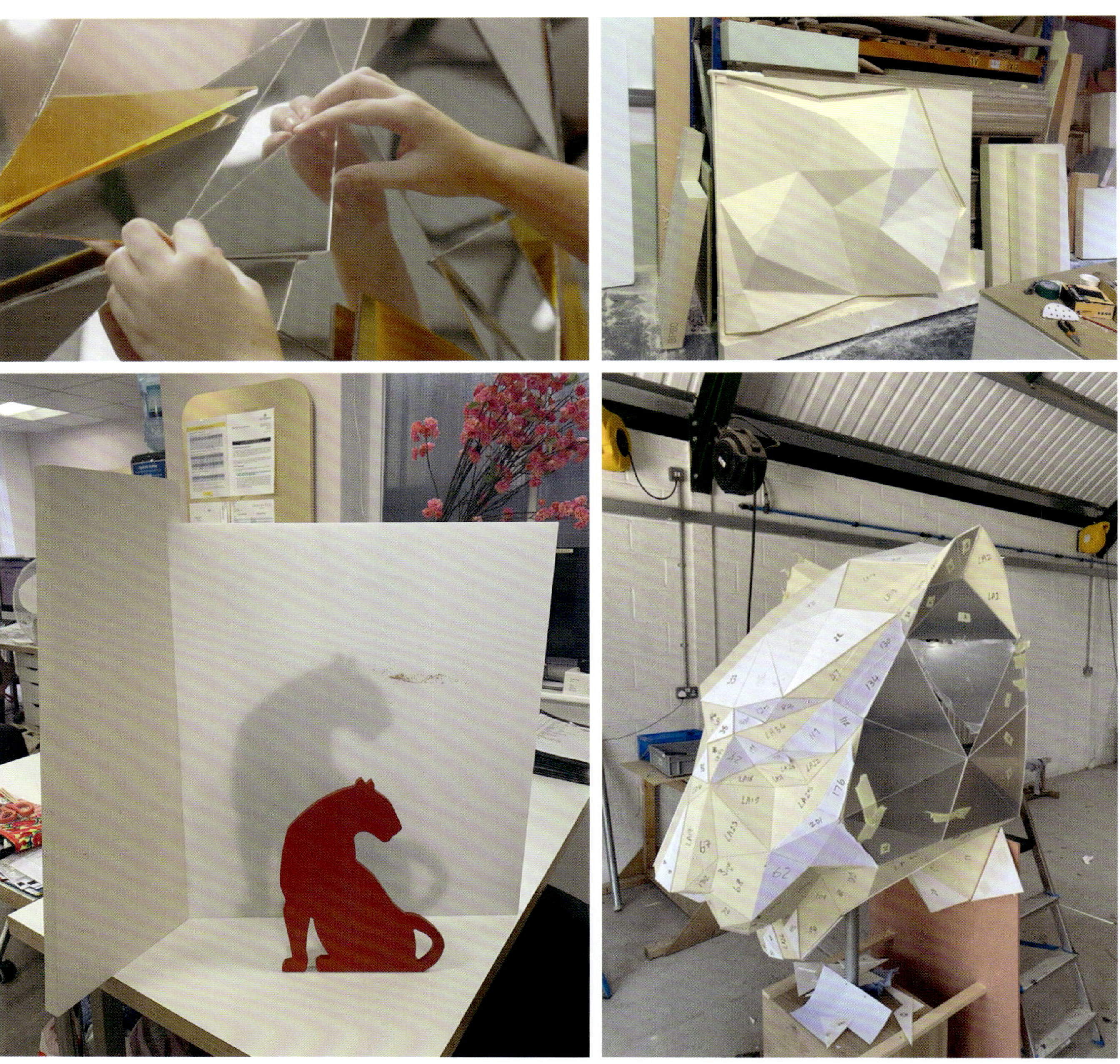

The complexity of this project lay in the diverse array of materials used from the Jeanne Toussaint–inspired emerald room's glass-tinted panels with programmed lighting revealing the designer's quotes to the floating pyramid mirrored screen with a sound system that beautifully narrated a story. The art installation in the window featured bespoke wallpaper, gold leaf and floating onyx, while the star of the show was the Panthère head, sculpted and covered with more than 200 pieces of glass to form a stunning multifaceted geometric face. The digital tunnel was a time-consuming labour of love as we worked alongside Cartier's Paris and London archive teams to select pieces that captured the history of the Panthère de Cartier in the most engaging, playful and memorable way possible.

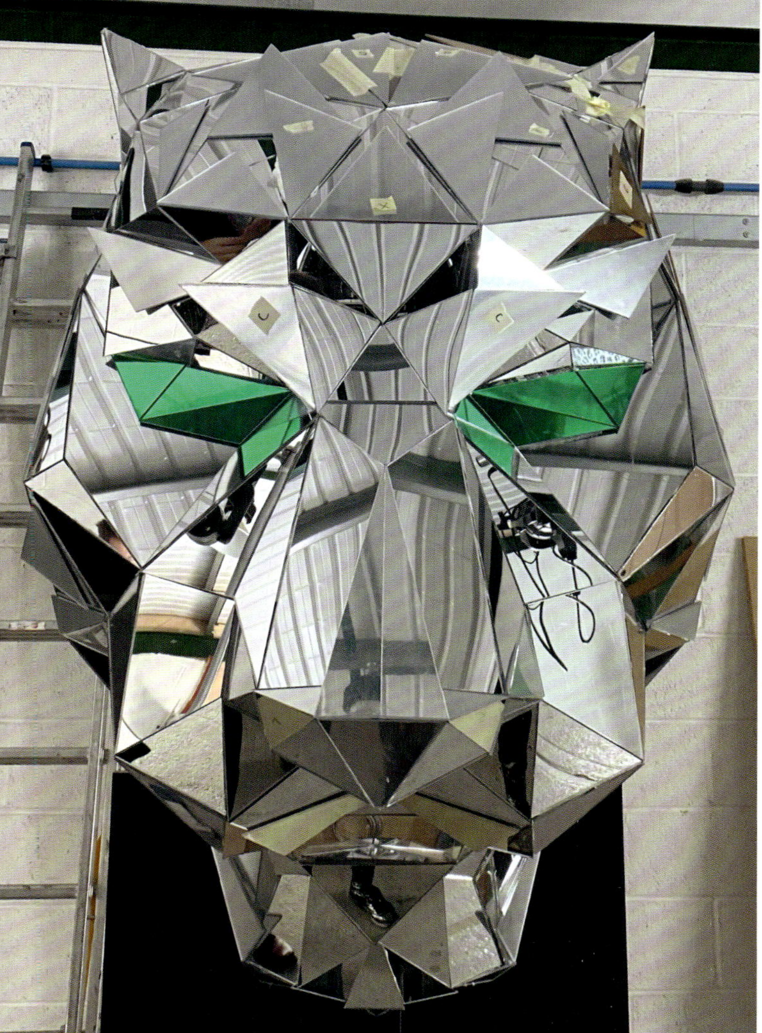

The most challenging part of this project was having to design during the Covid-related lockdown. Most of the design was done over Zoom meetings and phone calls while we were all under government orders to stay at home. This was the first project where we had to consider social distancing, Covid screens and general Covid safety into the design. The global pandemic also made material sourcing a challenge and sadly limited the pop-up's duration.

As with most of our projects, production materials were as sustainable as possible. Most of the elements from the pop-up were safely recycled and the rest were reused for other Cartier events, allowing the pop-up to be sustainable. This added a new dimension to the project and of course we wanted to ensure the features integrated well with the concept and didn't seem like an afterthought.

PANTHÈRE DE Cartier

PANTHÈRE DE Cartier
PANTHÈRE DE Cartier

Notwithstanding the limitations, the impact was remarkable. It was bittersweet to see it go, but the success and hard work invested in this project allowed us to translate the concept for the Saudi Arabian market. We love creating modern and impactful experiences that engage the visitors and ensure commercial success and brand awareness. Working closely with the Cartier team, we elevated our assets through digital and luxury art installations. This project was awarded an SBID Award.

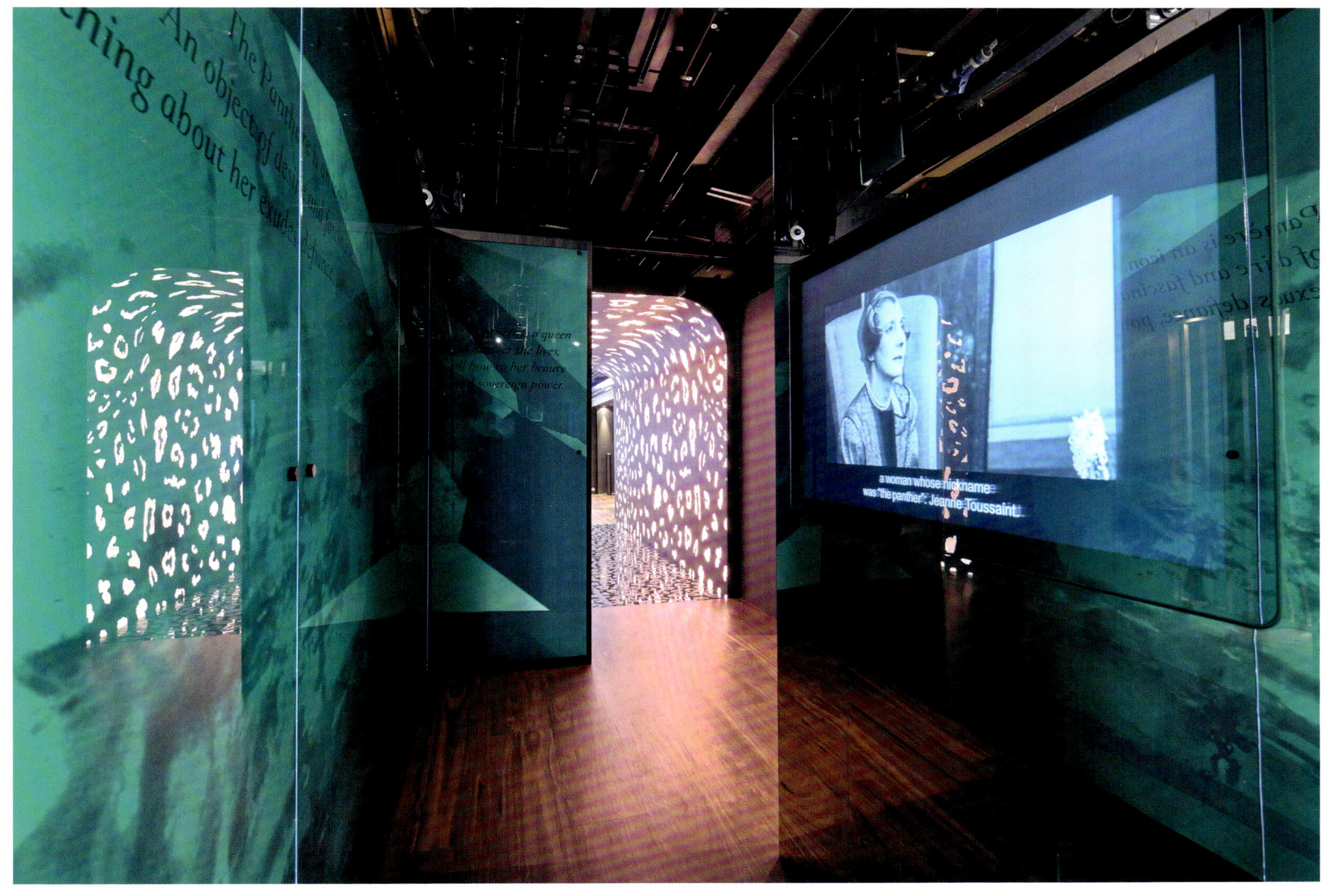

018285
CHAPTER 01
2017
On the Ronde Louis Cartier watch,
Cartier revisits the flamed techniq
and transposes it to gold, making it
a world premiere in watchmaking.
2017
2017
On the Revelation d'une Panthère watch, the wrists' movements cause a panther's head formed of a multitude of gold beads to appear or disappear. The piece explores the ancestral technique of the hourglass.

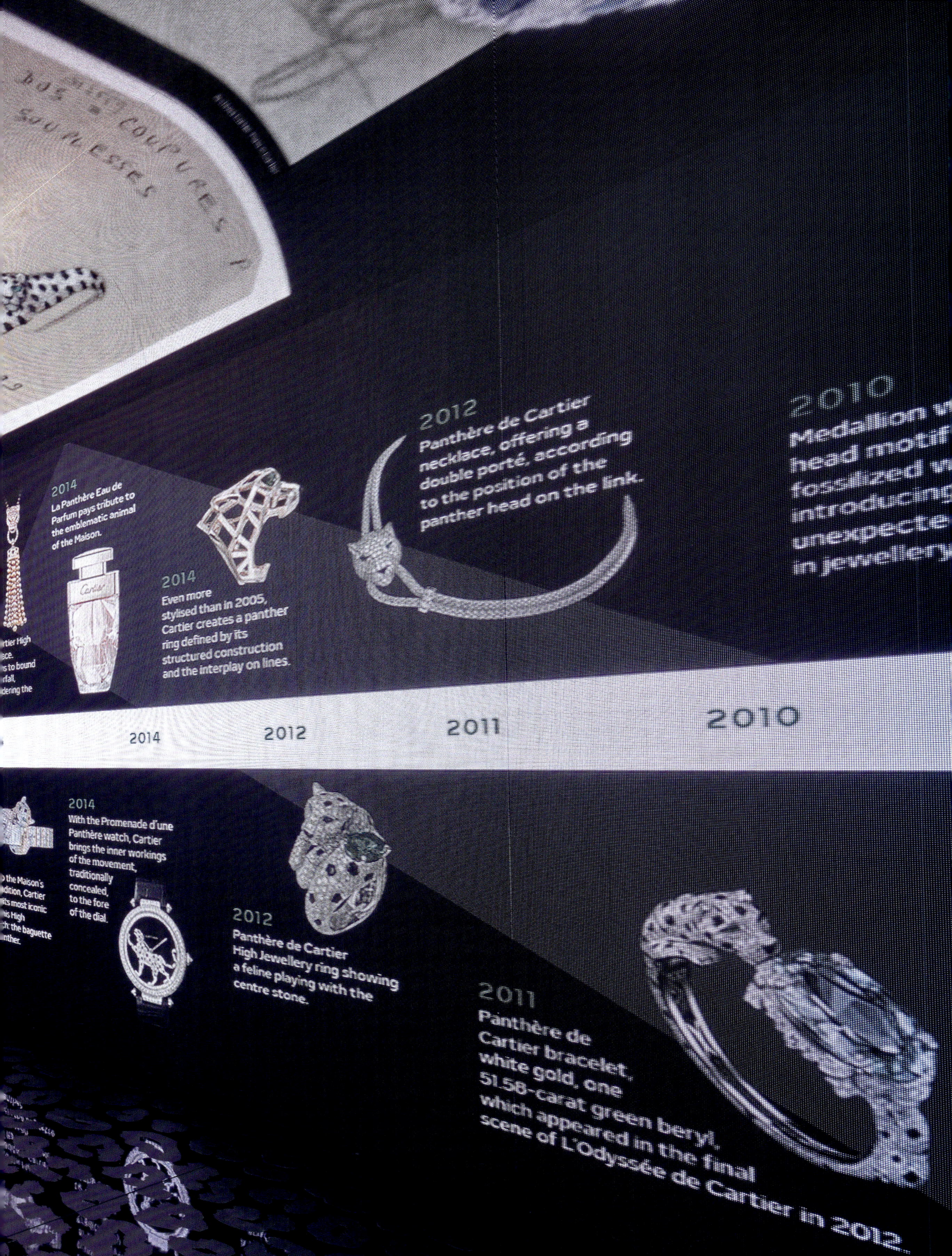
2012
Panthère de Cartier necklace, offering a double porté, according to the position of the panther head on the link.
2010
2014
La Panthère Eau de Parfum pays tribute to the emblematic animal of the Maison.
Cartier
2014
Even more stylised than in 2005, Cartier creates a panther ring defined by its structured construction and the interplay on lines.
2014
2012
2011
2010
2014
With the Promenade d'une Panthère watch, Cartier brings the inner workings of the movement, traditionally concealed, to the fore of the dial.
2012
Panthère de Cartier High Jewellery ring showing a feline playing with the centre stone.
2011
Panthère de Cartier bracelet, white gold, one 51.58-carat green beryl, which appeared in the final scene of L'Odyssée de Cartier in 2012.

PANTHÈRE DE Cartier

PANTHÈRE DE CARTIER—SAUDI ARABIA
CARTIER

Following the success of launching Panthère de Cartier in London at Harrods, the Cartier Middle East team seized the opportunity to expand into a new store, strategically located in front of their boutique undergoing refurbishment. The brief was therefore to adapt the successful concept for the Saudi Arabian market, creating a space that was both experiential and commercial. Half of the store was designed to offer an engaging experience, while the other half allowed customers to browse, touch, try and purchase their favourite pieces.

Riyadh / 2021

We cleverly reused the digital tunnel and its captivating content, designing a harmonious concept around these key assets. This approach ensured a seamless blend of interaction and commerce, tailored to resonate with the unique preferences and expectations of the Saudi market. The result was a space that not only showcased Cartier's exquisite Panthère collection but also provided an immersive experience that captivated visitors. Managing this ambitious project from Dubai while orchestrating efforts across teams in Saudi Arabia and London was a true testament to our organisational skills and the adaptability of our team. The complexities of Covid, coupled with travel bans and the observance of Ramadan, added layers of challenge that demanded innovative solutions and seamless communication.

Despite all the challenges, the project was a resounding success. What was initially planned as a two-month pop-up extended to six months, clearly demonstrating the durability and quality of our build. This longevity highlights our commitment to constructing pop-ups to the highest standards, ensuring they can stand the test of time and function as permanent installations if needed. This speaks to our craftsmanship and dedication to excellence in every project we undertake. This was also our inaugural project after establishing our official base in Dubai and it proved to be the ultimate test of our readiness to tackle the region's unique challenges. The experience fortified our resolve and sharpened our skills, ensuring that any future challenges are met with confidence and capability. Whatever hurdles may arise, we are now better equipped than ever to handle them with grace and efficiency.

PANTHÈ

DE Cartier

DIOR
MOVE YOUR HANDS

DIOR X KENNY SCHARF
DIOR

Dior tasked us with creating a visually stimulating, galaxy-style window installation to showcase Dior's Men's Pre-Fall 2021 joyful collection with its lively poppy prints inspired by the legendary surrealist pop artist Kenny Scharf. The project brief was clear: embrace the daring complexity and richness of mixed materials to create an environment bursting with colour and energy that marries the worlds of art and fashion.

Selfridges, London / 2021

Watch the video

The Dior/Kenny Scharf Corner Shop at Selfridges represented a vibrant fusion of pop art and high fashion. This project demonstrated our ability to navigate and overcome challenges with creativity and precision. Tasked with respecting Dior's vision of crafting an immersive galaxy-style space, we faced the formidable challenge of the corner shop's expansive windows and abundant natural light. We tackled this by employing a sophisticated mix of materials including printed bespoke carpet, lightboxes, mirror surface, lenticular and digital screens. The pièce de résistance was undoubtedly the floating monsters, suspended from the department store's ceiling, animated by a fan system. This installation not only adhered to the venue's stringent guidelines but was also executed within the tight time constraints. It was a harmonious blend of innovation and meticulous planning, reflecting our dedication to delivering exceptional experiences.

When you think you've seen it all, Dior comes around the corner with yet another surprise, offering new aesthetics and experiences. It's truly rewarding to collaborate with the Dior team, pushing boundaries together to consistently achieve beautiful and successful installations. The synergy and creativity that emerge from these collaborations are what make each project unique and memorable.

DIOR
AND

JOURNÉES SAVOIR-FAIRE
DIOR

Here we were asked to transform D or's New Bond Street store for the brand's Journées Savoir-Faire event, a live showcase for Dior's many craftspeople and artisans to show off their incredible skill and talent and offer guests a unique glimpse into the meticulous artistry that defines the House of Dior.

Dior New Bond Street, London / 2021

Our primary challenge was transforming the Dior store, renowned for its exceptional architecture and elegant, luxurious finishes, into an atelier that looked and felt authentic without altering or damaging the interior finishes and features. To achieve this, we opted for freestanding elements that respected both the integrity of the space and the stringent Health & Safety standards that are always our top priority. This approach not only preserved the elegance of the Dior environment but also enhanced it, offering an engaging, safe experience for visitors, allowing them to fully appreciate the artistry and distinctive savoir-faire for which Dior is celebrated the world over.

Participating in such an event is an honour and having the opportunity to meet the Paris team from the Dior Atelier was a remarkable experience. Discovering the beautifully intricate pieces from the Dior archive added an extra layer of magic to the event. Witnessing the awe on people's faces as they entered the enchanting space was incredibly rewarding. The surroundings framed the gorgeous pieces beautifully, creating an immersive and unforgettable experience. The transformation was truly remarkable, transporting visitors to the enchanted Dior Atelier, even if just for a moment.

"It's not just about sending a brief and waiting for a proposal. It's an open discussion, analysing the project together—materials, execution, alternatives. That's what makes [working with L'Atelier 5] special."

Luca Albero, Visual Merchandising Creation and Image Director, Dior

This installation was made with pre-loved straps
TANK

TANK BAR
CARTIER

We were tasked with designing, producing and installing a pop-up event along with accompanying window displays to celebrate the iconic Tank de Cartier watch and the launch of a vegan range of watch straps, a marriage of Cartier's heritage with modern values of sustainability.

Harrods, London / 2022

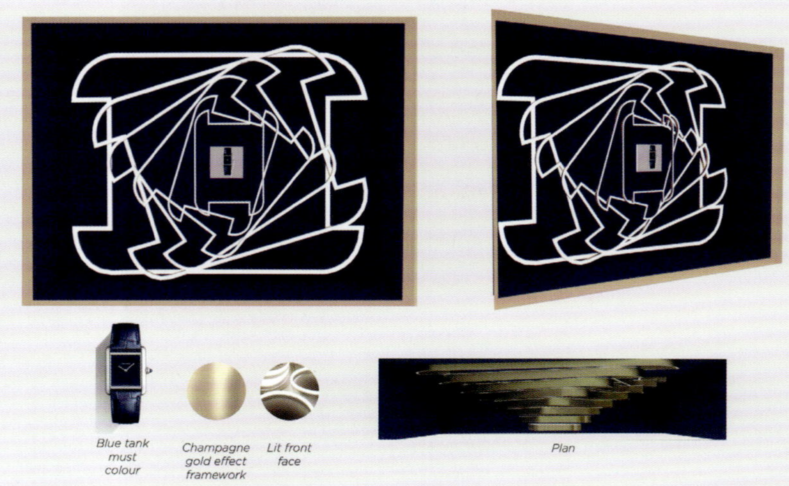

The experience featured four striking monochrome window displays at the Harrods boutique, a captivating art installation made from preloved watch straps and an immersive watch bar, blending retail theatre with refined craftsmanship to engage and delight visitors. Sustainability was key to this activation, as it follows the DNA of both Cartier and Harrods.

The Tank de Cartier has a legendary design that transcends time. We celebrated its hallowed status by creating a unique Tank strap bar for Cartier's Harrods flagship. Here, people were invited to choose and customise their straps with the Cartier team on hand to help find the perfect match. The window displays featured a striking monochrome art installation crafted from pre-loved straps, emphasising the brand's commitment to sustainability. This project required extra care as we were working with pre-loved watch straps. Each leather strap was painted to correspond to the perfect Pantone colour, creating harmony and respecting Cartier's iconic codes. This attention to detail ensured that the installation not only celebrated the timeless elegance of the Tank de Cartier but also aligned perfectly with the brand's aesthetic standards. This project beautifully combined heritage with modern values, creating an unforgettable experience.

"When you work with an agency on a project, they have to understand the house in terms of image and rendering, the quality of materials, refinement and the story we want to tell. At the same time, of course, it's not just an artistic exercise: they must also take into consideration the extreme value of the pieces on display."

Claire Meyssan, Special Projects Senior Manager, Cartier

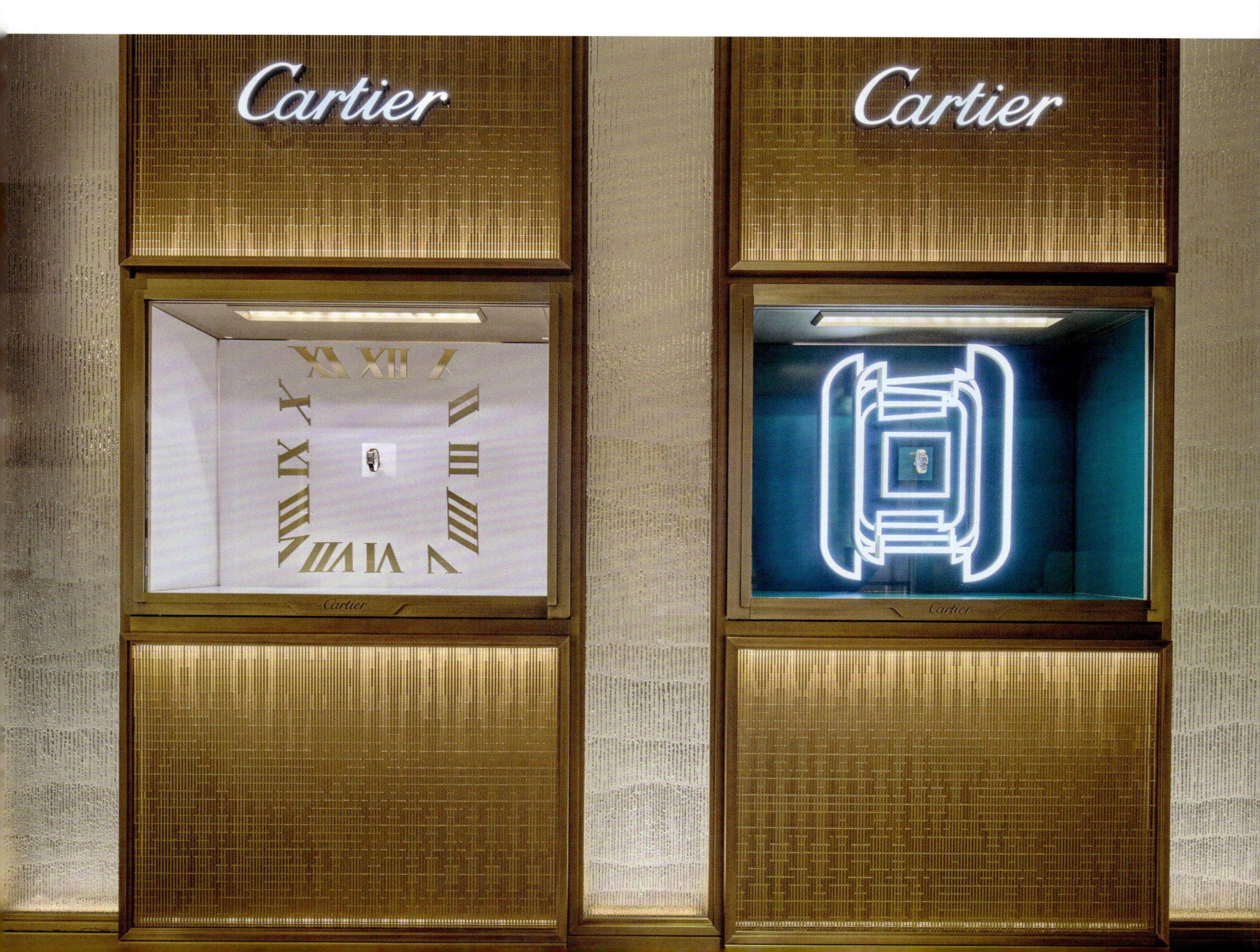

The artistic simplicity of the project, combined with the unmistakable codes—a combination of design elements, iconic symbols and brand heritage—of Maison Cartier created a naturally recognisable and elegant design. The beautifully designed strap bar, while serving as a practical commercial tool, offered an enjoyable journey for customers as they chose their favourite watch strap.

2. CHOOSE YOUR STITCHING COLOUR
This installation
was made with
pre-loved straps
1. CHOOSE
YOUR STRAP

tier
3. CHOOSE YOUR LINING & ENGRAVING

POSSESSION
Ramadan Kareem

RAMADAN—TIME TO TURN PIAGET

Our brief was to design, produce and install a contemporary, culturally sensitive visual merchandising display for the Ramadan windows that honoured Piaget's brand signature while referencing local culture and landscapes. Our design also needed to connect seamlessly to Piaget's marketing campaign to ensure a cohesive 360-degree brand experience. Additionally, we explored opportunities to enhance the concept through the flagship store façades, creating a striking and immersive Ramadan celebration.

Dubai, Abu Dhabi, KSA, Qatar, Bahrain, Kuwait / 2022

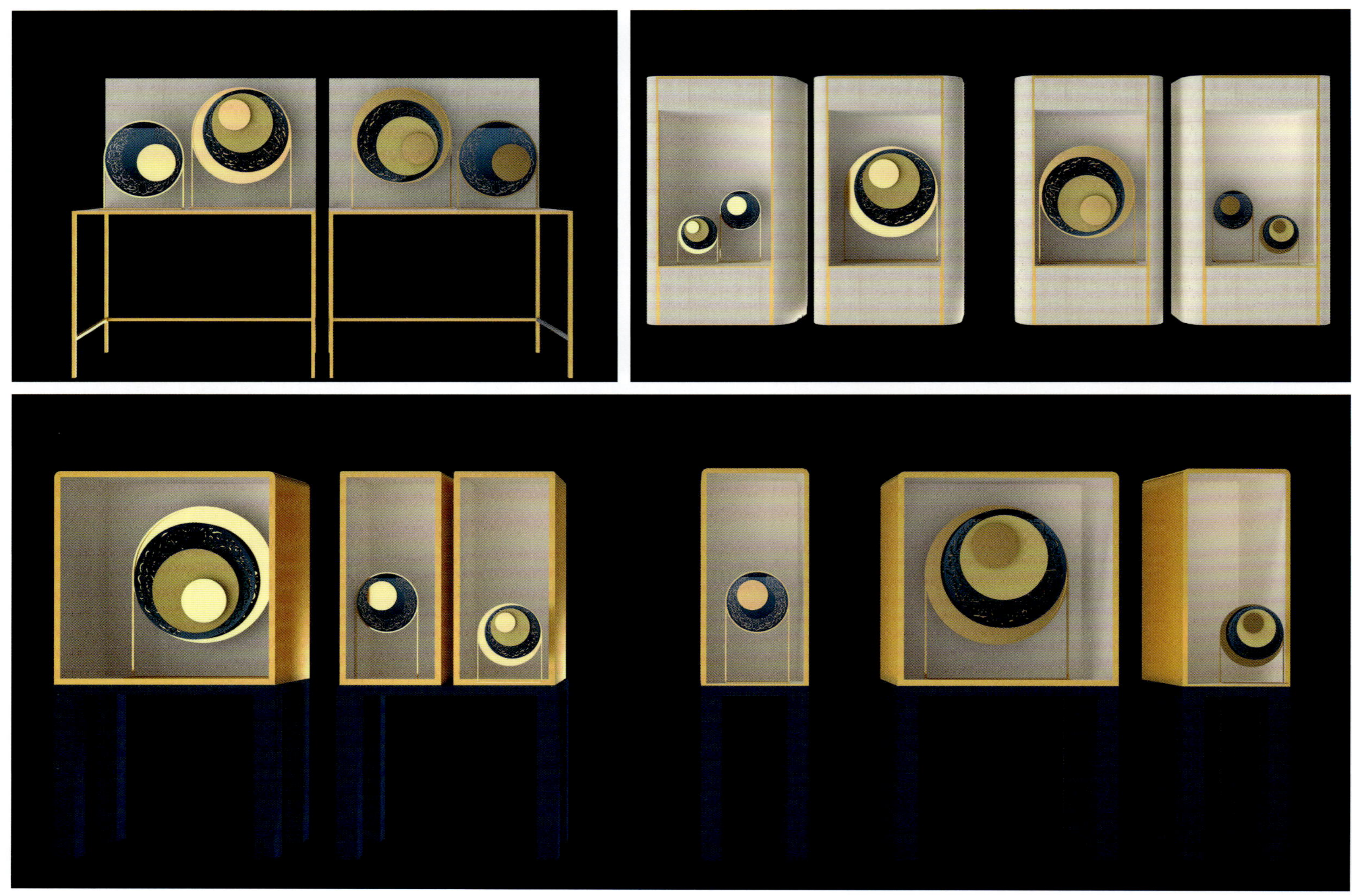

The essence of Ramadan is a month-long celebration rooted in reflection, community and generosity. We were acutely aware of the logistical challenge of sending everything to six separate locations so close to such an important period, especially on a very tight timeline. Overcoming this hurdle was achievable thanks to our team's efficiency and coordination. Successfully managing the logistics in such a time-sensitive context showcases our ability to adapt and deliver, ensuring that every detail is in place for the project to shine. It's moments like these that highlight the strength and resilience of our team.

It's a joy to witness luxury brands embracing the spirit of Ramadan, allowing us to create narratives that honour its significance with elegance and respect. Working on a Ramadan campaign holds a special place in our hearts. The values of reflection, community and generosity align beautifully with our own ethos as a creative agency making our involvement profoundly meaningful. The opportunity to weave these themes into our work not only enriches our creative journey but also strengthens the bond with our diverse audiences. It's a reminder of the power of storytelling and the universal language of compassion and connection.

"Saina is a very emotionally connected person. She loves people, she loves their energy and she genuinely cares about her team and her clients. I think people respond to that."

Sarah Metalnikoff, Operations Manager, L'Atelier Five Dubai

"Saina keeps a tough face publicly but she's actually one of the most caring and warm people I know."

Charlotte Adam, Senior Project Manager 2020–2022, L'Atelier Five

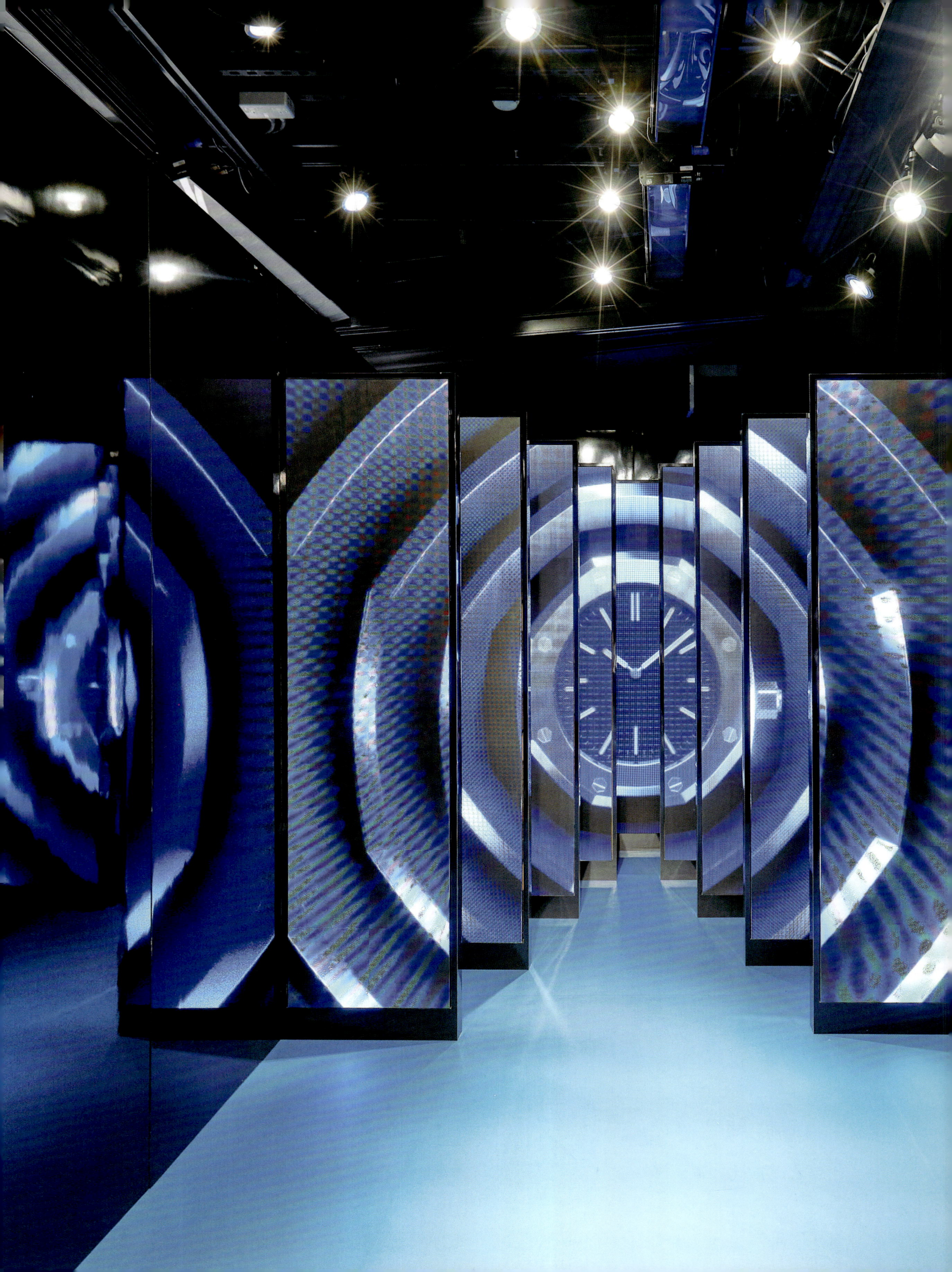

ROYAL OAK 50TH ANNIVERSARY EXHIBITION
AUDEMARS PIGUET

To celebrate the 50th anniversary of its iconic Royal Oak model, Audemars Piguet tasked us with creating a dedicated space at Harrods that would encapsulate the heritage of innovation and artistry of the Royal Oak and reflect its timeless elegance. The mission was to develop an immersive, impactful interactive concept that aligned with Audemars Piguet's brand ethos with a futuristic look and feel using materials and colours that echoed the codes of the Royal Oak collection. The key message revolved around celebrating a half-century of uncompromising design and forward-thinking vision. The aim of the space we designed was to invite visitors to enter the world of Audemars Piguet and discover the collection within an artistic and futuristic environment. This was also to be an experimental space, encouraging exploration rather than commercial transactions, thereby encouraging the store's customers to experience the product and understand the story behind it rather than simply view a timepiece.

Harrods, London / 2022

Watch the video 

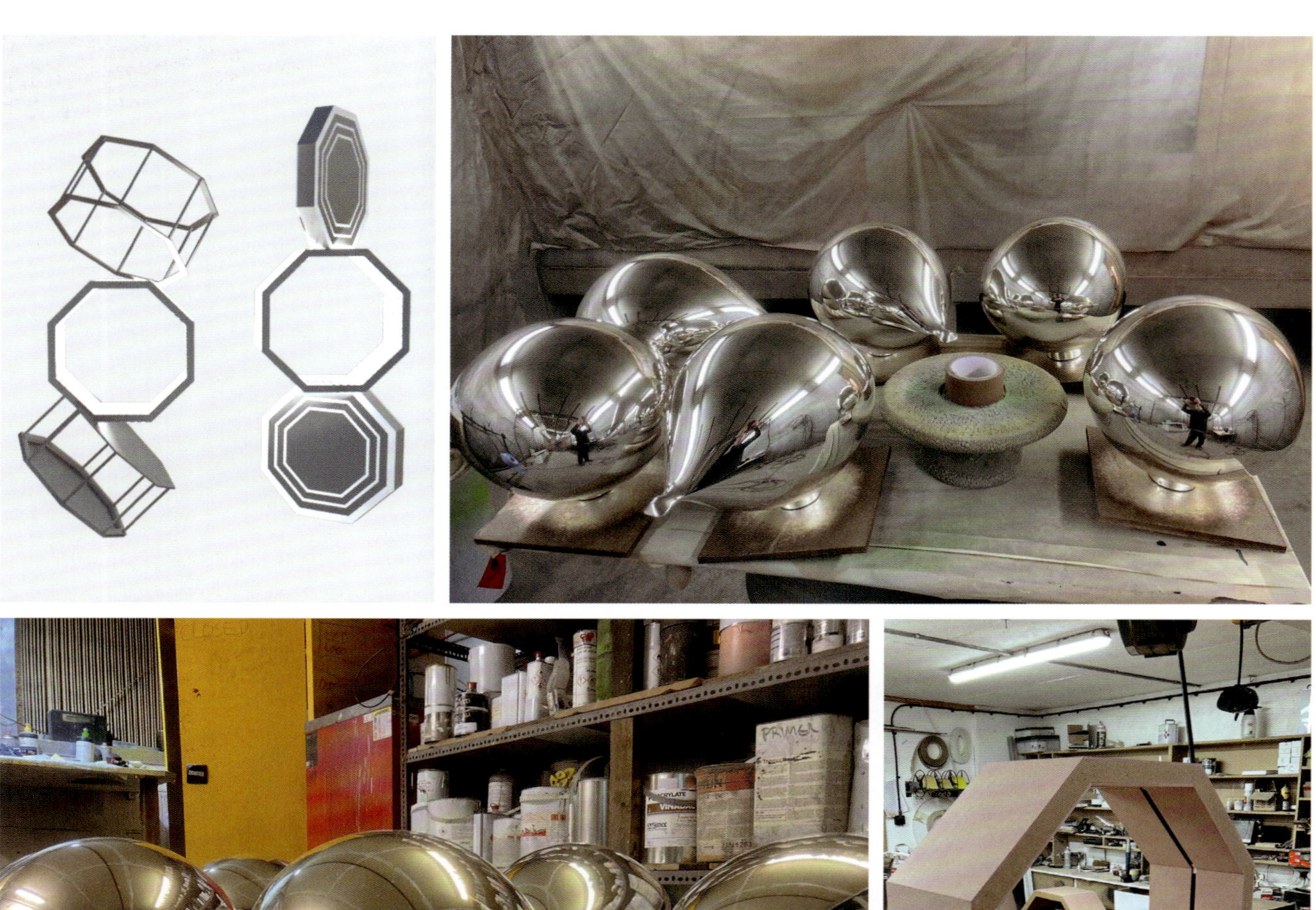

This was more than just another pop-up. It was a journey through time, showcasing the daring spirit and boundary-pushing innovation that defines the Royal Oak. As a brand, Audemars Piguet is known for pushing boundaries of watchmaking. The overall challenge was therefore to have an impactful creative concept, one that the brand had never attempted before. The key message revolved around the brand's uncompromising, forward-thinking ethos. Our team used angles, digital walls, hanging screens and floating chrome balloons along with the crowning achievement, an octagonal display unit—a feat of engineering accomplished in a remarkably short timeframe. This intricate structure required a blend of technical prowess and artistry. Witnessing this ambitious vision come to life was a testament to our team's technical expertise, collaborative spirit and unwavering commitment to excellence.

The goal of any pop-up is to leave a lasting impression, something astonishing that people will talk about and feel compelled to experience. Working alongside a team renowned for pioneering complex watches with such a rich heritage sets expectations high and places an even higher bar for execution. This collaboration not only demanded excellence but also inspired us to push our own boundaries and deliver beyond what was anticipated. For us, it presented a remarkable opportunity to grow stronger and more knowledgeable, leaving a lasting impact on our team.

"I was always attracted to the creative world but never thought of myself as 'creative.' In fact, for the longest time, I thought I was bad at it until I realised one day that being resourceful is a way of expressing creativity and I'm good at being resourceful."

Saina Attaoui, Founder and Managing Director, L'Atelier Five

CHRISTIAN DIOR
PARIS
EXCLUSIVITY

THE FABULOUS WORLD OF DIOR
DIOR

We were asked to bring to life "The Fabulous World of Dior," a full-scale holiday window takeover and holiday pop-up at Harrods. The aim was to transport visitors into a couture-inspired, whimsical, sensory experience. To achieve this, we created a breathtaking gingerbread-inspired wonderland where every detail—down to the last icing-like flourish—felt irresistibly edible, creating an atmosphere of pure festive magic.

Harrods, London / 2022

Watch the video

The Dior team had a clear vision of what they wanted and how they wanted it executed. To achieve their vision, we designed and constructed a whimsical gingerbread factory complete with a realistic-looking working mechanical conveyor belt. Achieving the gingerbread finish required months of meticulous testing and innovation to ensure the most realistic and luxurious gingerbread finish. Our team also experimented with sugar coating, icing, meringue making and caramel wheels to strike the perfect balance between artistry and craftsmanship while fulfilling strict venue guidelines and Health & Safety regulations.

"The Fabulous World of Dior" evoked a wide range of emotions to capture the magic of Christmas in a way that only Dior could. The project will be remembered for many reasons not least of which the fact that a few visitors actually tried to eat the walls! For us, one of the most satisfying aspects of this project was the opportunity to collaborate with a large team of talented and skilled artisans. Trusting in each other's expertise was key to achieving the exacting level of execution expected by our client. We were genuinely proud to be part of such a captivating and memorable experience.

CHRISTIAN DIOR
PARIS

"Saina is very warm but at the same time is tough, with the strength to hold her own in any situation. It's inspiring to work for a female leader who's achieved what she has in a male-dominated industry."

Stephanie Gomm, Project Manager, L'Atelier Five

"I don't believe I would have built this business if I had followed a traditional path of business of luxury studies."

Saina Attaoui, Founder and Managing Director, L'Atelier Five

HARRODS
CHRISTIAN DIOR

JACQUEMUS

BAMBINO ART INSTALLATION
JACQUEMUS

For this project, we were engaged to create a striking oversized version of Jacquemus' Bambino bag—a piece that would not only serve as a statement sculpture but also as a functional retail display for the brand's iconic collection.

Dubai Mall, Dubai / 2023

In the world of Jacquemus, where fashion meets art, every detail tells a story. Crafted from raffia and limewash paint, the Bambino bag is an example of true craftsmanship. Each raffia strand was meticulously attached by hand, one by one, transforming the structure into a tactile objet d'art. Moreover, our design team cleverly integrated product shelving, Jacquemus branding, a freestanding mirror and built-in lighting, creating a visually impactful and immersive brand experience. The interplay of natural textures and soft illumination evokes the sun-drenched landscapes of the South of France, grounding the installation in the brand's origins while elevating it to luxury status. While the finished piece exuded effortless elegance, its creation was anything but simple.

The first challenge was engineering a seamless structure that could be split to navigate the narrow access lifts and loading bays, all the way to its final destination in-store. Every element had to be meticulously designed to ensure not just aesthetic perfection but also logistical feasibility. But the real test came with the material itself. Raffia—a natural, organic fibre—posed a series of hurdles that would daunt even the most seasoned in the industry. To meet stringent fire safety regulations, the entire stock of raffia had to be fire-rated, an intricate process that hardened the material and subtly altered its colour to a darker hue. This required further tweaking to ensure the final look stayed true to the brand's vision. Each strand of raffia was then pressed to eliminate its natural curl, cut to precise lengths and applied by hand in a process that can only be described as haute couture craftsmanship. The result is a testament to the art of problem-solving in luxury design—a piece that is as much about technical mastery as it is about storytelling.

This project celebrates the harmony of form and function, where every element—be it the organic flow of the raffia or the strategic placement of the shelving—was thoughtfully considered. It also celebrated the power of human collaboration. Working closely with Jacquemus' Paris team and the local venue in Dubai, ideas flowed seamlessly, challenges were tackled together and every individual brought their expertise to the table. This was the key to achieving a result that was greater than the sum of its parts. We've always believed that great teamwork is the ultimate recipe for success. It's not just about delivering a project; it's about creating something that resonates, something that feels alive. And this installation, born from collaboration and shared passion, is proof of just that.

JACQUEMUS

THE CATENE COLLECTION DESIGNED IN MILAN
SPECIAL SELECTION AT INTERNATIONAL A' DESIGN AWARD & COMPETITION
BRONZE
2024

FROM MILAN TO HARRODS
POMELLATO

We were asked to create a multisensory experiential retail activation for Milanese heritage brand Pomellato that would resonate with both loyal admirers and new customers alike. At its heart, the activation aimed to attract new customers, spark brand discovery and draw visitors to the boutique. In this case, we opted for an exhibition-style design both visually striking and welcoming, offering an invitation to visitors to explore the essence of Pomellato's craftsmanship and immerse themselves in its timeless allure. Every detail had to be carefully curated to reflect the brand's identity, from the bold aesthetics of its iconic pieces to the contemporary elegance that has redefined fine jewellery. Our aim was to weave Pomellato's heritage with its modern vision, creating a connection that would linger long after the visit.

Harrods, London / 2023

Watch the video

Bringing Pomellato's world to life required more than just creativity—it demanded an unwavering commitment to precision and innovation. This project wasn't just about creating a visually stunning space; it was about elevating every element to the level of a permanent shop fit, ensuring the installation resonated with the brand's luxury identity. The space itself presented a unique challenge, divided into four distinctive aesthetics. Each required a bespoke approach, from custom flocking in precise Pantone shades for the displays to a printed carpet that tied the design together seamlessly. The gallery structure, with its programmed lighting, became a dynamic centrepiece, while the development of the personality test synchronised with digital content added an interactive layer to the experience. One of the most captivating features was the Nudo workshop table—a display showcasing the tools and elements used in the making of Pomellato's iconic collection.

This tactile and educational element of the workshop table brought the artistry of the brand to the forefront, inviting visitors to connect with Pomellato's craftsmanship on a personal level. The final challenge was perhaps the most intricate: integrating the existing hoarding into the installation. By dressing it in Pomellato's signature Pantone colours and incorporating their latest chain design, the hoarding became an extension of the installation itself, blending seamlessly into the overall aesthetic. Every detail demonstrated the meticulous craftsmanship and problem-solving that define our approach. From the lighting to the materials, each element was thoughtfully designed to ensure a cohesive, luxurious experience that not only reflected Pomellato's heritage but also pushed the boundaries of experiential design.

"Saina understands that it's important to not limit yourself at the start of the project so she encourages us to 'think big' creatively. But, she already has a 360-degree view of the project with all its limitations and challenges so if we go too far, she knows exactly when to step in and guide us back without clipping our wings."

Rafael Roe, Designer, L'Atelier Five

The final result of the Pomellato activation was nothing short of extraordinary. From the moment visitors stepped into the space, it was clear that Pomellato had successfully transported its Milanese heritage to the heart of Harrods. The design beautifully showcased the brand's iconic collection, creating a space where craftsmanship and elegance took centre stage. The activation wasn't just a visual treat—it was a journey of discovery. Visitors were drawn in, engaging in meaningful conversations and exploring the stories behind Pomellato's bold and modern designs. The personality test, a standout feature, became an instant success, sparking curiosity and creating a deeper connection with the brand. Its impact extended far beyond Harrods, carrying through to different markets and continuing to captivate audiences, even in Asia. This project is a testament to the power of thoughtful design and storytelling. It created a seamless fusion of heritage and innovation, leaving a lasting impression on shoppers and solidifying Pomellato's place as a truly exceptional fine jewellery brand.

Pomellato
NUDO

From Milan
To Harrods
ATELIER
Nudo crafted

THE
DALMORE
HIGHLAND SINGLE MALT SCOTCH WHISKY
AGED 21 YEARS

HANS CRESCENT TAKEOVER
THE DALMORE

For The Dalmore 21 launch, we were asked to conceptualise, produce and install a cohesive series of seven unique window displays for the iconic Hans Crescent windows at Harrods to reflect the bold, distinctive aesthetic and celebrate The Dalmore's heritage, craftsmanship and contemporary elegance. Beyond the windows, the project extended to a permanent wall bay in the wine shop and an exclusive rooftop event. These elements taken together were intended to create a dynamic touchpoint for engagement—offering a lasting feature in-store and a memorable brand experience. Taken together, the elements were intended to showcase the world of The Dalmore's new brand in a way that was as innovative as it was elegant.

Harrods, London / 2023

Watch the video 

The primary challenge was achieving precision in the alignment of angles and lighting to create a seamless interplay of shadows, ensuring the design's visual depth and impact were fully realised. Meticulous attention was also required to develop the perfect gradient of colours, carefully calibrated to enhance the perspective and mirror the rich, golden tones of the whisky. Golden and amber tones inspired by the whisky's essence were brought to life through light, mirrors and bespoke acrylic gradients, creating a poetic interplay of reflections and shadows. A connecting light line wove together the seven windows, while playful perspectives and infinity effects added depth and intrigue. This demanded a highly engineered approach, combining advanced lighting techniques and custom acrylic fabrication to achieve the desired The Dalmore gradient. The execution was a masterclass in modern design—sleek and luxurious with a particular focus on the bottle as the central element of the display.

Collaborating with The Dalmore team was an absolute delight and their embrace of the 'less is more' philosophy aligned beautifully with our vision. The execution was sleek, refined and undeniably luxurious, making the final result something we're incredibly proud of. Seeing The Dalmore take over Harrods in such an elegant and impactful way was a powerful moment for us. Harrods holds a special place in our hearts, and witnessing a brand grow its activation within such a prestigious space is always deeply satisfying. It's a reminder of why we do what we do—to create moments that resonate and leave a lasting impression.

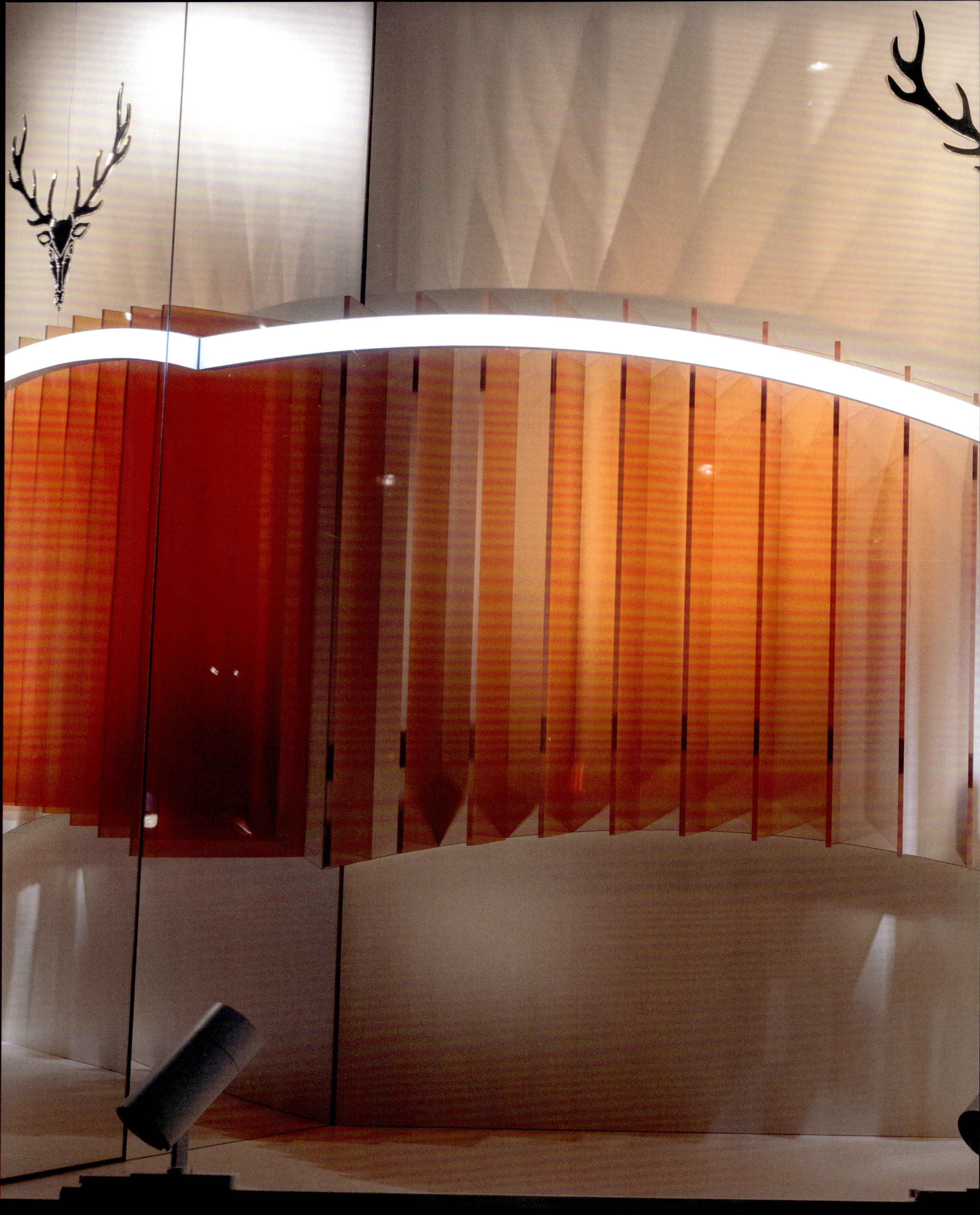

L'OCCITANE
EN PROVENCE
L'OCCITANE
EN PROVENCE
GiftsForEveryone
L'OCCITANE
EN PROVENCE

HOLIDAY ACTIVATION—WISHING TREE
L'OCCITANE

We were entrusted by L'Occitane to design an interactive pop-up installation for their holiday retail activation that brought to life their iconic ingredients and rich brand history. Designed to captivate and engage, the installation aimed to create an immersive, sensory journey. Every detail was carefully curated to evoke the essence of Provence, reimagined with a bold, retro twist. Our starting point was a palette of warm hues that evoked Provence of the 1970s. Married with the playful textures and patterns of the era, we managed to create a space that radiated nostalgia whi e staying unmistakably modern.

Dubai Mall, Dubai / 2023

The pop-up was destined to be installed in the heart of Dubai Mall, a bustling public space where thousands pass through daily. Our biggest challenge was clear: to create an engaging pop-up that paid a heartfelt tribute to the landscapes, scents and traditions of Provence where visitors could explore, interact and capture moments to share with friends, family and the world but, just as importantly, meet all the local Health & Safety regulations to ensure public safety. Working closely with our structural engineer, every element was designed and produced to withstand the unpredictable—whether it was children climbing the tree or someone mishandling the installation. At the heart of the activation, we created a captivating photo opportunity—an artfully crafted centrepiece that drew visitors in and invited them to become part of the story. Every detail, from the materials used to the structural integrity of the installation, was carefully considered and tested to ensure it remained not only safe but also visually impeccable throughout its duration. Whether the whimsical interplay of light and shadow or the tactile details inspired by nature, every element encouraged exploration and interaction. And, we're happy to report that from day one to the very last, the pop-up stood as a testament to thoughtful design and engineering expertise.

This installation was more than a visual spectacle. It elevated the customer experience and enhanced brand awareness, leaving a lasting impression. By bridging the past and present, it created a moment of connection—a celebration of Provence's heritage viewed through a fresh, contemporary lens. For Saina, working with L'Occitane always feels deeply personal. As someone from the South of France, this collaboration is a way to honour her roots and share the beauty of Provence with the world. There's a sense of pride in promoting a brand that embodies the essence of a region so close to her heart, one that celebrates its heritage with authenticity and elegance.

TANE
ENCE

AMIRI
AMIRI

AMIRI

LET YOUR STAR SHINE—HOLIDAY WINDOWS
AMIRI

We were commissioned by Amiri, a modern American West Coast luxury brand, to design holiday windows and in-store pop-in activations for their holiday campaign. Amiri effortlessly marries the rebellious spirit of Los Angeles with the meticulous craftsmanship of haute couture. When tasked with translating this spirit into a retail space, we imagined a narrative woven around a journey through the sun-soaked streets of California, where grit meets glamour. We designed the space to transport visitors into a world where denim tells a story, where leather carries a legacy and where every corner whispers the tales of artisans who pour their soul into their work. Our aim was to create a space that felt like an extension of Amiri's identity, something honest, something real.

Atlanta, Chicago, Houston, Las Vegas, Los Angeles, New York, Tokyo, Shanghai, Dubai / 2023

While every great design project begins with a vision, it is the meticulous execution that transforms it into a successful retail experience. For us, the challenges of crafting a bespoke retail experience across far-flung places added an additional level of complexity. From space accessibility and architectural constraints to power availability and consistency of materials, execution became a delicate dance between creativity and practicality, artistic vision and technical expertise, where no element—no matter how small—could be left to chance. In this instance, the project was managed by our team in Dubai and involved problem-solving, late-night adjustments and the relentless pursuit of perfection across multiple time-zones to bring the vision to life. Mastery of these challenges is precisely what makes our execution of work extraordinary.

Collaborating with Amiri for the first time was an honour and a tremendous responsibility, which we embraced wholeheartedly. Despite the challenges—navigating time zones, adapting to diverse spaces and maintaining consistency across multiple locations—we're proud to say the outcome was overwhelmingly positive. The campaign resonated worldwide, a testament to the synergy between Amiri's bold vision and our dedication to storytelling through design. This collaboration stands for us as a reminder of what we can achieve when trust is placed in creativity and craftsmanship. It's a milestone that inspires us to continue pushing boundaries in the world of luxury retail.

76
AMIRI

AMIRI

BHR
DON PAPA
RUM
DON PAPA
RUM

WELCOME TO SUGARLANDIA POP-UP
DON PAPA

We were asked to design and build an engaging and immersive pop-up experience that both educated visitors and elevated brand awareness for Diageo's Don Papa brand of aged dark rum. Through captivating storytelling, the activation was designed to bring Don Papa's DNA and values to life in an enticing and intriguing way. The pop-up invited travellers to explore the brand's rich, mysterious world and convert them into new customers.

Charles de Gaulle Airport, Paris / 2024

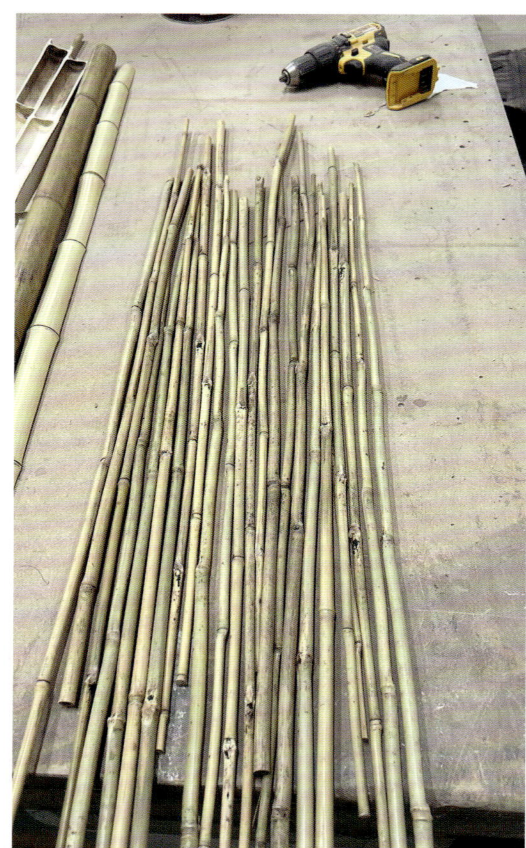

Working on airport installations always present unique challenges; however, our team now has extensive experience in this domain such that we're able to navigate them smoothly. In this instance, the main challenge we encountered resulted from incorporating materials like bamboo and sand into our designs. However, our resourcefulness and expertise ensured that we successfully met such challenges. When it comes to Health & Safety, clear rules are our guiding stars. As long as we respect these guidelines, we can find innovative ways to comply while maintaining our creative vision. This balance between creativity and compliance is what allows us to deliver exceptional and safe installations every time.

Witnessing the pop-up come together in such a controlled environment was truly satisfying and the response from travellers was incredible! This impactful activation not only captivated the audience but also showcased our ability to create compelling experiences that resonate with people from all walks of life. It's moments like these that highlight the power of thoughtful design and creativity in transforming spaces and engaging audiences.

DON PAPA
POUR TOUT ACHAT
D'UNE BOUTEILLE DE
DON PAPA
RECEVEZ UNE
FLASQUE
Welcome

DON PAPA
POUR TOUT ACHAT D'UNE BOUTEILLE DE
DON PAPA
RUM
RECEVEZ UNE FLASQUE
Sugarlandia

LA PRAIRIE
SWITZERLAND

Swiss luxury cosmetics brand La Prairie engaged us for the launch of their new La Prairie Caviar Mist collection in Dubai. Our team designed and organised an elegant open-air activation event blending contemporary luxury with local sophistication. Set at Lucky Fish, an exclusive Mediterranean restaurant and terrace overlooking the Dubai waterfront, this select open-air activation embodied elegance and vibrancy. Guests were treated to a multisensory experience with bespoke cocktails, gourmet canapés and a sophisticated soundtrack enjoyed against a breathtaking backdrop of stunning sunsets over turquoise seas framed by branded elements.

Lucky Fish & Achievher Studio, Dubai / 2024

Watch the video

A successful live event is all about precision, planning and preparation. Every detail, from guest arrivals to the flow of drinks, canapés and service by the iconic Caviar Boy must be flawlessly coordinated. It's about foreseeing every scenario, ensuring the photographer and videographer are ready and creating seamless moments—whether it's an intimate workshop or a photo opportunity. Each element must harmonise like music to deliver an experience that resonates with guests and everyone involved.

Our team arrived the morning of the event from a project installation in Korea, jetlagged but determined. Despite the whirlwind, everything came together beautifully, proving that with the right preparation, even the most ambitious events can be a resounding success.

The launch of La Prairie's Caviar Mist was nothing short of spectacular—a summer event that embodies the kind of experience we'd love to create time and time again. From the breathtaking setting to the seamless coordination, everything came together beautifully. The reception was a resounding success. Here's to more unforgettable moments like this!

LA PRAIRIE
SUMMER CLUB

水井坊
水井坊
Shui Jing Fang
外销
SPECIAL SELECTION AT INTERNATIONAL A' DESIGN AWARD & COMPETITION
BRONZE
2025

INCHEON MULTI-BRAND SHOP-IN-SHOP
DIAGEO

We were selected by global drinks giant Diageo to design, build and install a luxurious multi-brand airport retail space at Incheon Airport in Seoul. Our aim was to create a sleek, sophisticated space in which to immerse travellers in the essence of Diageo's world of fine spirits and premium drinks brands. Every detail required meticulous craftsmanship to achieve a timeless design—one that not only honours Diageo's rich legacy but also looks boldly to the future. We sought to design an immersive environment that would serve as a dynamic platform for storytelling, product discovery and exclusive activations, seamlessly blending elegance with cutting-edge innovation.

Incheon Airport, Seoul / 2024

Watch the video

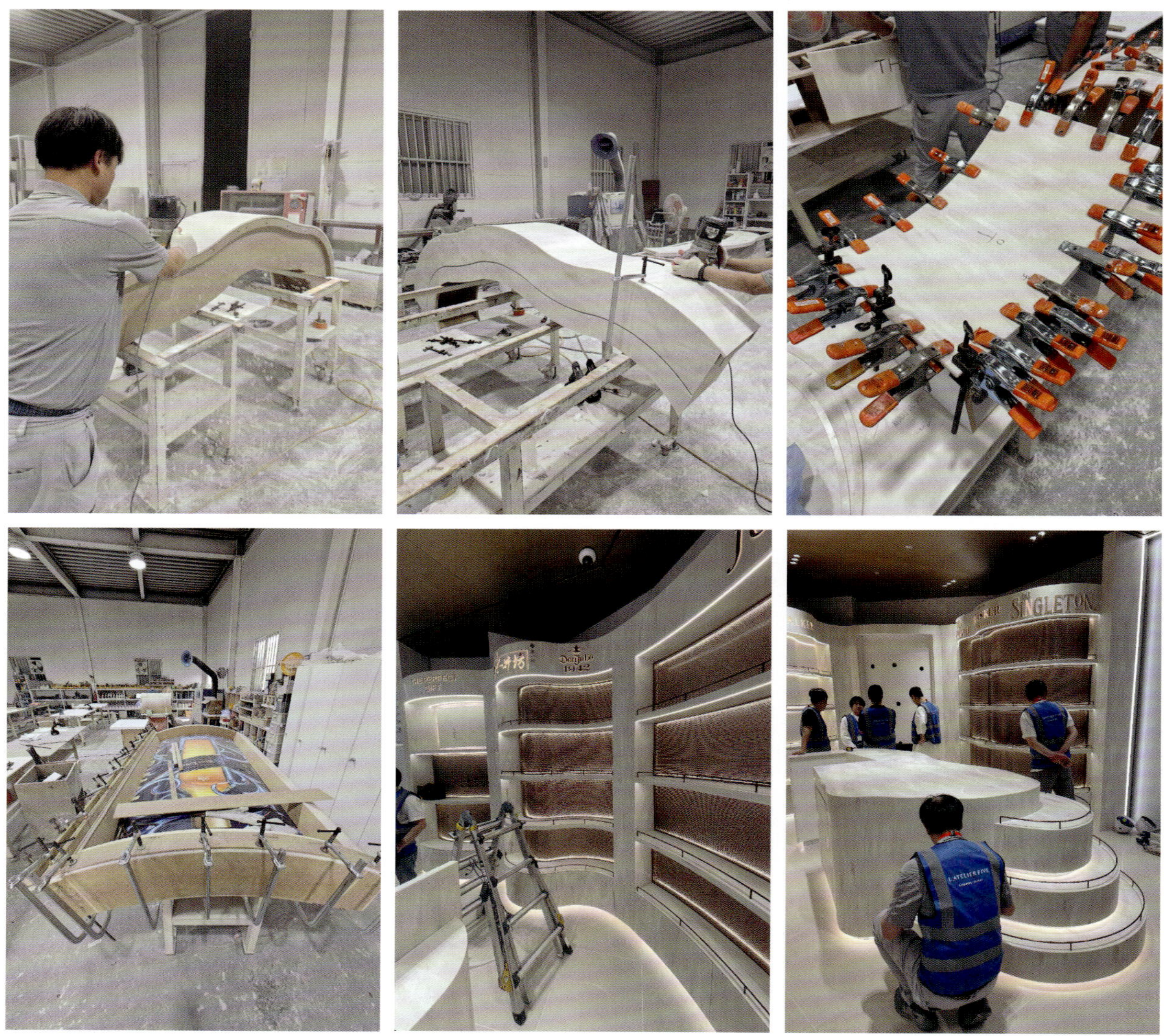

While the creative vision was developed in London in close partnership with Diageo's UK office, project management and technical production were expertly handled by our Dubai team so as to ensure swift responses across multiple time zones. Mock-ups and production visits saw the team travelling between London, Dubai and Seoul, ensuring clear communication and teamwork at every stage. The production took place in Seoul and adhered to strict airport security guidelines. From overcoming language barriers to managing logistics in a high-security environment, every detail was coordinated with precision. The engineering of the curved Corian, heat-bent to perfection, achieved a floating, smooth aesthetic with seamlessly covered joint lines. Integrated lighting was designed to look natural, while bespoke perforated panels reflected the brand's distillery heritage with meticulous detail. The result was a flawless execution that blended luxury with technical excellence, a testament to the power of collaboration across continents and cultures.

The Korea project truly exemplifies our global reach and collaborative spirit. Designed in our London office and expertly project managed by our Dubai team, the production came to life in Korea, showcasing our seamless integration across continents, cultures and languages. This international collaboration reflects our commitment to delivering bespoke retail experiences that transcend geographic boundaries, ensuring innovation and excellence at every stage. It was a process we thoroughly enjoyed, a wonderful example of the power of teamwork and our dedication to crafting unforgettable moments.

THE PERFECT
GIFT

NNIE WALKER
GLETON
JOHNNIE WALKER
Blue Label
XORDINAIRE
BLENDED SCOTCH
JOHNNIE WALKER
Blue Label
BLENDED SCOTCH WHISKY
TRAVEL
EXCLUSIVE

LONDON
DUBAI

A DECADE OF MAGIC

As I reflect on this incredible journey, I feel immense gratitude for the experiences, challenges and, most importantly, the people who have accompanied me along the way. Every project, collaboration and challenge have shaped L'Atelier Five into what it is today: a closeknit, family-style agency thriving on creativity, passion and the relentless pursuit of excellence.

The past decade has been transformative, both personally and professionally. The industry has evolved from traditional visual merchandising to immersive pop-ups, in-store events, and full-scale brand takeovers. Today, we craft experiences that merge physical artistry with digital innovation, creating not just spaces but emotions. Luxury is ever evolving, a game of anticipation, where understanding social behaviour, politics and cultural shifts is crucial. One thing remains constant, however. The power of design to create desire, evoke emotion, and leave a lasting impact. It's a beautiful challenge that keeps us inspired and ready to adapt to the ever-changing luxury retail landscape.

At the heart of it all lies our client's brief. From that initial spark, we craft activations that are visually stunning and deeply relevant. We navigate timing, budgets and cultural nuances, ensuring every project resonates with diverse audiences while staying true to the brand. A significant part of our work lies in the details. Luxury comes alive in the craftsmanship, artistry and human touch. Collaborating with local artists has been one of the most rewarding aspects, enhancing storytelling and celebrating the beauty of craftsmanship.

Throughout this journey, I've had the privilege of meeting incredible artists, designers, marketing directors, project managers, craftspeople and visionary leaders. Each has taught me something valuable. I believe in treating everyone with respect, care and compassion. Building trust and long-lasting relationships is about giving the best service possible but also elevating others along the way. These connections have been a cornerstone of my growth, both personally and professionally.

Being a woman in a male-dominated industry has been challenging at times but empowering as well. This journey demanded resilience, determination and belief in my vision. I've faced many obstacles but learned that with focus, sacrifice and drive, anything is possible. Knowledge is power, and I've immersed myself in learning and growing every step of the way.

If I can offer one key lesson I've learned it is that you can't do everything by yourself. Surrounding yourself with talented, passionate people fuels your growth. Creativity thrives on interaction with others; immerse yourself in it and watch it flourish.

I was told my dreams were unattainable, too risky or not fit for me as a woman or mother. I chose to transform those doubts into strength. I stepped out of my comfort zone, focused on my career and aligned myself with the luxury values of the world's best brands making them the cornerstone of L'Atelier Five. Craftsmanship, attention to detail and bespoke service are at the heart of everything we do.

This book is more than a celebration of L'Atelier Five's achievements. It's a testament to the power of dreams, hard work and collaboration. It's a tribute to the talented individuals who helped bring our visions to life and the brands that entrusted us with their stories. Together, we've created something meaningful, inspiring others to dream big and push boundaries.

To those starting their journey, I can't tell you that it will be easy. There will be challenges, doubts and sacrifices to make. But, if you believe in something deeply enough, your passion, resilience and hunger for knowledge will enable you to reach your goals. It hasn't been easy for me, but I have no regrets. I believe that it's better to follow your gut, trust yourself and take the leap. If you fail, you pick yourself up and try again, smarter this time. The saying 'we live and learn' couldn't be truer. Every setback, every lesson has brought me closer to where I am today. Find your passion, put everything into it and never give up. The road may be tough, but the reward of pursuing what you truly love is worth every step.

As we close this chapter and look to the future, I feel profound excitement. The journey is far from over. Surrounded by a powerhouse of talent, I'm inspired to continue creating, innovating and pushing the boundaries of luxury design.

Here's to the next decade of magic! May we keep dreaming, designing and innovating—together.

With immense gratitude,
Saina Attaoui,
Founder, L'Atelier Five

A SPECIAL DEDICATION TO MY SON, MYLO

Throughout this entire adventure, there has always been one constant, one unwavering source of strength—my son, Mylo. L'Atelier Five is just eighteen months older than him, and from the moment he came into my life, he has been my greatest motivation, my fuel, my everything.

Every late night, every challenge, every obstacle I have faced, I've done it with him in my heart. I've fought to build this agency not only to create something extraordinary but to give him a great example. To show him that no matter the circumstances life throws at you, you can rise above it, you can persevere, and you can achieve greatness. I've wanted to be the best version of myself, not just for me, but for him—to prove to him that with passion, determination, and resilience, anything is possible.

Today, Mylo has grown up alongside L'Atelier Five. He is our biggest supporter, cheering us on every step of the way. And what fills me with even more pride is how he gets involved from time to time, bringing his fresh, young Gen Z perspective to the table. His ideas, his energy, his curiosity—they remind me why I started this journey n the first place.

A little anecdote that always brings a smile to my face: when we moved to Dubai five years ago to open L'Atelier Five Dubai, Mylo was captivated by the beauty of the region. The stunning architecture, the modernity, the impeccable service—it all left a mark on him. Since then, he has dreamed of becoming an architect, inspired by the very city that became a second home to us. Watching his passion and ambition unfold fills me with so much pride, and I can only hope for a bright and incredible future for him.

It hasn't been easy at all times, but I could not wish for a better companion. Mylo has always been so understanding and respectful of my long hours, hectic travel schedule, late nights, and multiple events. He has been admiring and supportive of the work I do, always cheering me on as my biggest supporter and fan. Thank you, Mylo, for being so wonderful and understanding. You are such a special person, and I hope you always keep dreaming big my love.

While this journey has been challenging, I would do it all over again for him. I am a fighter, and I will always fight for him. Mylo, you have given me a strength I didn't know I had, and for that I am endlessly grateful. Thank you for being my light, my inspiration and my greatest joy.

Watch this space, because with you by my side, the future is limitless.

With all my love,
Mum

ACKNOWLEDGEMENTS

This book is a celebration of the artistry, creativity and passion that defines L'Atelier Five. It has been made possible through the collective efforts of our talented team, collaborators and the inspiring brands we have had the honour to work with. It also marks a milestone in a journey that has not been without its challenges but has remained undeniably beautiful and deeply inspirational. It stands as a testament to the power of resilience, female empowerment and the boundless potential of young artists. May it inspire dreamers to believe in their visions and pursue their careers with courage, passion and unwavering determination.

This project was a leap into the unknown for us. We could not have done it without the guidance of a talented group of dedicated professionals. Our heartfelt thanks to the writers, editors, book designer, photographers, photo editors, make-up artists, stylists, hair and make-up artists who helped us pull this book together and bring it to life. Thank you!

Here's to the family we have built and the magic we continue to create together.

Concept and Creative Direction
Guiding the magic with vision and heart:
Saina, Rafael, Anya, Sarah, Luke, Jasmine

Design Team
The dream makers of L'Atelier Five who carefully craft beauty, one detail at a time.
Jasmine, Stephanie, Claire, Rafael, Anya

Our Beautiful London Team
You bring creativity, passion and love into everything we do. You are the foundation of our journey. Your dedication and brilliance make every project shine brighter.

To those team members who have moved on, know that you remain forever part of our L'Atelier Five family. Thank you for your contributions, your memories and the legacy you have left behind. You remain with us in heart and spirit.

Project Managers
The orchestrators of excellence who turn dreams into reality with precision and care.
Sophie, Charlotte, Daria, Stephanie, Kosha

PA, Finance and Operations Team
The skilled administrative wizards behind the magic who keep everything running smoothly.
Kris, Hallia, Camille, Audrey

Our Beautiful Dubai Team
Your unwavering dedication, resilience and ability to push through, despite the time difference and distance, inspire us every day. You are the heart of our global operations and your tireless efforts bring our vision to life in the most extraordinary ways.
Sarah, Claudie, Tiffany

The Little Joy Makers
A heartfelt thank you to the children and pets who fill our lives with love and laughter.
Mylo, Raphaël, Aryan, Noah, Maximilian, Rose, Takis, Nala, Kobe and Duchess

Our sketch artists
The talented artists who bring L'Atelier Five to life, one sketch at a time.
Dimitri Theocharidis, Alice Nyong

ACKNOWLEDGEMENTS

Storytellers Behind the Lens
Capturing the magic, one frame at a time.
Yinka Williams, Stefan Weil, Warren Dupuy, Luca Piffaretti, Austin Hutton, Martyn Hicks Photography, Tim Barratt, Abstract Iron, Craig Gibson, Sungbeon Kang, Tiberiu Cosneanu, Sandeep Mathur, Xavier Ansart, Pal Production, Wolf Entertainment

Creativity Behind the Portraits
Fashion Sourcing: @SovrceLvxe Styling: Lia Ningiza / Fashion Assist: Rina Sakurai / Hair and Makeup: Hakim Elhocine. PP 16 and 54: Jacket and Trouser by Nadine Merabi, Glasses by Chanel, Shoes by Christian Louboutin; P 21: Top and Skirt (Exclusive Pieces) by Katie Ko, Shoes by ALAÏA, Earrings and Bracelet by Lugano Diamonds; PP 27 and 40: Jacket and Trouser by GUCCI, Shoes by Christian Louboutin; P 32: Top and Skirt (Exclusive Pieces) by Lizandro Acera, Hat by Emily London, Shoes by Prada, Earrings, Rings and Bracelet by Lugano Diamonds; PP 35 and 46: Top (Exclusive Piece) by Lizandro Acera, Trouser by Gucci, Shoes by Christian Louboutin, Earrings by Lugano Diamonds; P 43: Skirt by Del Core, Shoes by Christian Louboutin, Bracelet and Rings by Jenny Bird; P 62: Dress (Exclusive Piece) by Katie Ko, Shoes by Alevi Milano.

Production Partners
L'Atelier Five is built on the foundation of long-term partnerships with whom we share a dedication to excellence. Their technical expertise and unparalleled attention to detail transform every challenge into an opportunity, even under the tightest timelines. It is their incredible talent, dedication and ingenuity that make the impossible possible. Together we are strong, crafting extraordinary experiences that leave a lasting impact and inspire creativity for generations to come.

Artists, Artisans and Collaborators
Since its inception, L'Atelier Five has sought out talented artists, artisans and craftspeople. To the painters, sculptors, poets, and craftspeople of all types, whether your medium is raffia, paper, wood, metal, fibre glass or language, your tremendous skill and passion enable us to bring whimsy and joy to our projects and elevate the experience for everyone involved. Thank you for helping us bring even our most ambitious challenges to life with grace and purpose.

Our Visionary Clients
To the luxury brands who entrust us with bringing their vision to life, we are endlessly grateful. Your confidence in us and your passion for what you do in turn fuel our creativity and inspire us to push boundaries. It continues to be an honour to craft bespoke experiences that reflect your unique heritage and values. Together, we have created magic that captivates and connects with audiences worldwide. Thank you for being an integral part of the L'Atelier Five journey. Here's to many more years of innovation, partnership and unforgettable moments!

This book is a celebration of the power of collaboration, creativity and the art of storytelling. Thank you for being part of our journey.

With gratitude and admiration,
The L'Atelier Five Family

L'Atelier Five Ltd.
8 De Walden Court
85 NEW CAVENDISH STREET
LONDON, W1W 6XD UNITED KINGDOM
contact@latelierfive.com
TELEPHONE +44 (0)20 7491 8181
www.latelierfive.com
@latelierfive

L'Atelier Five FZ-LLC
Design District D3
Building 3, Floor 3
P.No: SD4-015
Dubai, United Arab Emirates
sm@la5dubai.com
TELEPHONE +971 58 524 2230
www.la5dubai.com

Published in Australia in 2025 by
The Images Publishing Group Pty Ltd
ABN 89 059 734 431

Offices

Melbourne
Waterman Business Centre
Suite 64, Level 2 UL40
1341 Dandenong Road
Chadstone, VIC 3148
Australia
Tel: +61 3 8564 8122

New York
6 West 18th Street 4B
New York, NY 10011
United States
Tel: +1 212 645 1111

Shanghai
6F, Building C, 838 Guangji Road
Hongkou District, Shanghai 200434
China
Tel: +86 021 31260822

books@imagespublishing.com
www.imagespublishing.com

The Images Publishing Group Reference Number: IM1759

A catalogue record for this book is available from the National Library of Australia

Title: L'Atelier Five: Contagious Creativity by L'Atelier Five
ISBN: 9781923094024

This title was commissioned in IMAGES' Melbourne office and produced as follows:

Interviews, Project Direction, Editorial Direction and Design lbd-hnl
Cover Design L'Atelier Five
Creative Direction Nicole Boehringer
Editorial Jeanette Wall
Proofing Holly Alexander
Production Simon Walsh, Heather Johnson

EU GPSR Authorised Representative: Easy Access System Europe Oü
Company Registration ID: 16879218 | Address: Mustamäe tee 50, 10621 Tallinn, Estonia
Email: gpsr@easproject.com | Tel: +358 40 500 3575

Printed on 157gsm Zunma matt FSC paper in China by C&C Offset Printing Co., Ltd.